140TH OPEN CHAMPIONSHIP
Card of the Championship Course

Hole	Par	Yards	Hole	Par	Yards
1	4	444	10	4	415
2	4	417	11	3	243
3	3	240	12	4	381
4	4	495	13	4	459
5	4	419	14	5	547
6	3	178	15	4	496
7	5	564	16	3	163
8	4	453	17	4	426
9	4	412	18	4	459
Out	35	3,622	In	35	3,589
			Total	70	7,211

2011

Happy Christmas Dad
All my love.

Carl xx
Samuel + Luke
x

Based in St Andrews, The R&A organises
The Open Championship, major amateur
events and international matches. Together
with the United States Golf Association,
The R&A governs the game worldwide,
jointly administering the Rules of Golf,
Rules of Amateur Status, Equipment
Standards and World Amateur Golf Rankings.
The R&A's working jurisdiction is global,
excluding the United States and Mexico.

The R&A is committed to working for golf
and supports the growth of the game
internationally and the development and
management of sustainable golf facilities.
The R&A operates with the consent of
143 organisations from the amateur and
professional game and on behalf of over
thirty million golfers in 128 countries.

Aurum Press
7 Greenland Street, London NW1 0ND

Published 2011 by Aurum Press

Statistics of the 140th Open Championship produced on an IDS Computer System

Assistance with records and research provided by Malcolm Booth, Alastair Buchan,
Peter Lewis, Fiona MacDonald, Salvatore Johnson, and www.golfobserver.com

Course illustration by Graham Gaches

A CIP catalogue record for this book is available
from the British Library

ISBN-13: 978 1 84513 679 6

Designed and produced by Davis Design
Colour retouching by Luciano Retouching Services, Inc.
Printed in Great Britain by Purbrooks

THE OPEN CHAMPIONSHIP

WRITERS
Andy Farrell
John Hopkins
Lewine Mair
Art Spander
Alistair Tait

PHOTOGRAPHERS

Getty Images
Stuart Franklin
Scott Halleran
Ross Kinnaird
Streeter Lecka
Andrew Redington

The R&A
David Cannon
Matthew Lewis
Warren Little
Ian Walton

Golf Editors
Justin Davies
Rob Harborne
Richard Heathcote
Richard Martin-Roberts
Steve Rose

EDITOR
Bev Norwood

The Championship Committee

CHAIRMAN
Jim McArthur

DEPUTY CHAIRMAN
JR Jones

COMMITTEE

Paul Baxter	Stuart Lloyd
Alick Bisset	Richard Souter
Tony Disley	Richard Stocks
Martin Ebert	Donald Turner
Stuart Graham	David Wybar

CHIEF EXECUTIVE
Peter Dawson

DIRECTOR OF RULES AND EQUIPMENT STANDARDS
David Rickman

Introduction

By Jim McArthur

Chairman of the Championship Committee of The R&A

This year at the 140th Open Championship we paused to remember that the world of golf had lost one of its greatest players and special personalities, Severiano Ballesteros. His passion for golf and indeed life itself was there for all to see, and it was appropriate that we honoured his memory.

Once again Royal St George's proved itself as a true Open Championship test. We wish to thank the Captain, Edward Demery; the Championship Committee Chairman, Richard McLean; the Committee and the Members for hosting the Championship and, indeed working with us to provide a Championship to remember.

The players all commented on the spectacular condition of the golf course, and for that our thanks go to Course Manager/Head Greenkeeper, Graham Royden and his staff.

Also we could not have staged the Championship without the thousands of volunteers who come from all over the world, some year after year, to perform various tasks.

Our congratulations go to the Champion, Darren Clarke, whose persistence for 20 years in this competition has resulted in him becoming only the second Open Champion from Northern Ireland and the first since Fred Daly 64 years ago.

We hope this Annual will be an enjoyable reminder of a memorable week.

Foreword

By Darren Clarke

Winning The Open has been a dream of mine since I was a kid, and it feels incredible to have done it. It's been a long and bumpy road. Good things and bad things have happened to me. Now it's pretty amazing, looking back on it all.

I have to thank my Mum and Dad and my fiancée Alison. I have been with my manager, Chubby Chandler, since 1990, and I cannot thank him enough.

I also know there is someone watching from above, and I know Heather would be very proud of me. But I think she would be more proud of our two boys, Tyrone and Conor. What's important now is that when I got home the boys had the Claret Jug in their hands and they could see their dad's name on the trophy.

As I say, it has been a long journey. I'm 42 and I'm not getting any younger, but I got here.

In Search of Another Hero

By Andy Farrell

When the Royal St George's Golf Club wrote their history, they called it *A Course for Heroes*. One look at the roll of honour from Opens past confirms this is no exaggeration.

There are, of course, the well-known names and they are certainly heroes, the likes of JH Taylor, the very first Champion, Harry Vardon and Walter Hagen, who both won here twice, Henry Cotton and Bobby Locke, Sandy Lyle and Greg Norman. But do not forget the likes of Jack White, of Sunningdale, in 1904, who bettered Taylor's score of 10 years earlier by 30 strokes and was the first man to finish under 300 for four rounds in an Open.

Then there was Reg Whitcombe, who battled through a gale in 1938, and two unsung heroes from America, Bill Rogers in 1981 and Ben Curtis in 2003. When Curtis won, on the first day there was a bit of a breeze. Only three players broke 70

and two of them were Norman and Davis Love III, old hands on the links. One player called it "mega tough," and that was from a Scot, a golfing breed who usually bang on about a "wee zephyr" when hats, golf balls, seagulls, and everything else are being blown out to sea.

Call that a gale? *This* is a gale, as Crocodile Dundee might have put it if he was actually from Dundee. In 1938, one of the most ferocious gales hit the last day of The Open, when two rounds were played. Whitcombe was one of only three men to twice break 80 with scores of 75, the best of the day, and 78. Meanwhile, the exhibition tent really was being blown out to sea.

"I was staying at a hotel on the sea front at Deal," wrote Henry Longhurst, "and I woke on the last morning with the curtains blowing in horizontally at the window. Outside, the sea was swishing and roaring and boiling and dashing itself against the promenade. I leapt out of bed and saw a really splendid gale blowing up." Alf Padgham drove the green at a hole of 384 yards and holed the putt for a 2, but the same length hole in the opposite direction required three mighty belts. "Fantastic

The clubhouse at Royal St George's.
Four bunkers circle the sixth green (preceding pages).

With the green set into hills, the third hole is the only par 3 on the Open rota without a bunker.

were the cries of woe told by some of the lesser fry," Longhurst added. Whitcombe survived, a hero indeed, if a very wet one as a torrential downpour started up as soon as the gale blew itself out.

The last Open at Sandwich was played in a heatwave on the Kent Riviera. Seasons seem to be magnified in this south-eastern corner of England. An east wind, even in May, perhaps especially in May, feels as if it has not paused for breath since departing the Siberian winter. Donald Steel, the writer and course designer, wrote: "It is easy to appreciate that golfers at Sandwich can be colder, wetter, and more miserable than anywhere else, but equally there can be a peace and serenity that transcends all else." All that applied again during the 2011 Open.

Bernard Darwin called Sandwich "perfect bliss" and popularised the attraction of the larks singing overhead. They still do. Amid the sand hills, glimpsing the sea at times, other players on other fairways only occasionally, not much appears to have changed since Darwin's time. Round and

about time marches on. One of the biggest wind farms in Europe stands out past Pegwell Bay. The huge Pfizer plant, where Viagra was conceived and developed, is unmissable, but to local dismay will be wound down next year as the company withdraws from the site. For the first time, highspeed trains delivered spectators from London St Pancras to the links in an hour and a half.

Inside the ropes the challenge of the course remains a subtly shifting one. This is perhaps the greatest compliment that its founders, Dr Laidlaw Purves and Henry Lamb, could be paid. Fed up of the mud tracks at Wimbledon and Blackheath, the pair set out to find a tract of land similar to that on which these two London-based Scots learned to love the game in their youth. Purves, legend has it, spied the dunes "with a golfer's eye" from the top of St Clement's church in Sandwich. He was right, and soon there were three thriving links, not just St George's, the name honouring the home of golf at St Andrews, but Cinque Ports at Deal and Prince's, which lies the other side of the 14th fairway.

If the Old Course at St Andrews has to be learned under every varying condition of the elements, so too St George's takes some knowing. Champions here tend to be those who plot their way around with caution. The list of Open winners includes master tacticians, as were Walter Travis, an American who won the Amateur Championship at his first attempt in 1904, and, of course, Jack Nicklaus. The Golden Bear won the St George's Grand Challenge Cup in 1959, although his experiences in Opens here were less rewarding.

Curtis was a rookie in 2003 who was the first player to register on the Saturday before The Open. He then did something very sensible. He went and talked at length to Andrew Brooks, the professional, and his assistants and got an instant insight into how the course plays differently in different winds. "A laser is no good here," Brooks said. "A hole might play differently just 10 minutes later with just a tiny change in the wind."

Curtis was the only player to finish under par, albeit his surprise victory was aided by the collapse of Thomas Bjorn in a bunker at the 16th. He took three blows to escape from the same trap that scuppered David Graham in 1985. Bjorn, who finished one back, had also received a two-stroke penalty on the first day for thrashing his club in the sand after failing to escape at the 17th.

You take what you are given at Sandwich. In 1993, summer rainstorms softened the course and the scoring was exceptional. Against one of the strongest leaderboards you could ever wish for, including Nick Faldo, Bernhard Langer, Nick Price, Corey Pavin, and a young

The tee shot on the fourth is challenged by the bunker in the face of the hill.

In the **Words** *of the* **Competitors...**

"

"I'm trying to go in here as though it's a first time. I'm trying to pretend I've never played here before and I'm just trying to learn it all from the start, from scratch."

—Phil Mickelson

"The biggest thing is controlling the flight of your ball, especially if the wind gets up, which it normally does here."

—Ben Curtis

"My first Open was here at Royal St George's (2003). I remember I led The Open after three holes and got such a fright when I saw my name on the leaderboard that was all I can actually remember."

—Charl Schwartzel

"Strategically it's a good golf course. You have to plan your way around it. It's not always driver off the tee, which is quite nice."

—Lee Westwood

"Every Open course offers different challenges. This one, some of the greens are a bit more severe than other Opens I have played. Some of the hardest holes have some of the hardest greens, and some of the easier holes have some of the flatter greens."

—Luke Donald

At 381 yards, the 12th is the shortest par 4, but the fairway has mounds, hollows, and bunkers.

Ernie Els, Norman won with a closing 64, the lowest score ever to win an Open. "I never missed a shot," he said. Gene Sarazen, the 1932 Champion at Prince's, said: "I never thought I'd live to see a Championship like it."

Langer, who returned to The Open this year after winning the 2010 Senior Open Championship at Carnoustie, had been close in 1981 and 1985. On the Saturday night in 1993, the German explained why it was best not to tangle with the out of bounds to the right of the par-5 14th. On Sunday, his challenge faltered when he ended up on Prince's. Even as resolute a mind and as deliberate a thinker as Langer had been confounded.

Sandwich can be awkard and ungainly. It is unsettling, especially in comparison to mighty links such as Royal Birkdale and Muirfield, the way the fairways roll and wander around and hillocks get in the way. It is a legacy of the "sporty" design favoured by Purves. Alterations have been going on ever since, with even Darwin, who wished not to change a thing about the place, admitting that the "whole art of golf did not consist of hitting a ball over a sand hill and then running up to the top to see what had happened on the other side."

Among the changes since 2003, four new tees added 100 yards to the course, but the most anticipated alterations were the widening of the first, 17th, and 18th fairways to provide more secure landing areas. Eight years earlier, only just over a quarter of the field managed to hold those fairways. Meanwhile, the fourth hole, with its huge bunker facing the players as they drive off, was made a par 4 from the same tee where it was deemed a par 5 in 2003. The total par for the course was therefore returned to 70 from 71.

One feature that was left well alone was Duncan's Hollow. The depression to the left of the 18th green was where in 1922 George Duncan, who had won at Deal two years earlier, made a crucial error in his pursuit of Hagen, who was already being proclaimed the Champion in the London evening papers. Their

Round Royal St George's

No 1 • 444 yards Par 4
The fairway has been widened by 12 yards, but an accurate tee shot is still essential. The carry over the "Kitchen," the valley in the fairway, is 250 yards, while three bunkers short left of the green must be avoided with the approach to a green that slopes towards the back.

No 2 • 417 yards Par 4
Two bunkers guard the corner of the dogleg on a hole that sweeps right to left. The carry is around 250 yards, leaving a short iron to the green over a ridge. Miss the green anywhere and it will be a tricky chip back to the putting surface.

No 3 • 240 yards Par 3
The only par 3 on the Open rota without a bunker, but it does not need one. It is a monster now that 30 yards have been added off the tee. A long, narrow green is set into the hills, surrounded by thick rough, and features a pronounced step between the front and back tiers.

No 4 • 495 yards Par 4
Played as a par 5 in 2003 after the new tee was put in. Now back to a par 4 but from the same tee. The drive is challenged by the vertiginous bunker set into the face of the hill, while the green falls away sharply on the left, while putting up the bank on the right is no fun either.

No 5 • 419 yards Par 4
A dogleg to the left around the huge Maidens hill. John Daly and others have tried to drive the green in the past — it is a carry of 320 yards past the farthest dune — but a more cautious play is to find the flat part of the fairway for a view of the green between the sand hills.

No 6 • 178 yards Par 3
The Maidens hole itself, playing towards the big dune with a long, two-tiered green set below the ridge and angled at 45 degrees to the tee. Ten yards has been added to the tee, but clubbing here is notoriously difficult. Four bunkers circle the green to await anything offline.

No 7 • 564 yards Par 5
From the new Championship tee, 32 yards farther back, it is now 280 yards to the saddle that hides the fairway, which then bends to the left. Finding the short grass is essential to have a chance of an eagle or birdie, but the approach must not be over the green.

No 8 • 453 yards Par 4
Always a tricky hole, turning away from the seafront. The drive is uphill and must be to the left to avoid two bunkers on the right. The approach is then down to a long, two-tiered green with a bunker short left and another pinching the green on the right.

No 9 • 412 yards Par 4
A new tee adds 24 yards, but it is still a relatively short hole where accuracy is all-important. The fairway is highly undulating and controlling the tee shot is tricky, even without having to avoid a bunker left and two in the middle of the fairway. Four bunkers guard the green.

No 10 • 415 yards Par 4
Runs back in the opposite direction to the ninth and plays uphill to a raised green. Anything short will roll back, but an approach over the back is even worse, while there are two bunkers down on the left and another on the right. Double-bogey is a real risk if offline.

No 11 • 243 yards Par 3
Another long par 3, but this hole plays downhill and the prevailing wind is behind. A large green which makes putting a real challenge here. Whether going up or down the tiers or just negotiating the many subtle breaks, good green-reading skills are essential.

No 12 • 381 yards Par 4
The shortest par 4 on the course, but this dogleg left-to-right hole features another fairway that is tricky to negotiate with a number of mounds and hollows, plus three bunkers early on the fairway and five more up towards the green for the more adventurous.

No 13 • 459 yards Par 4
Although straighter and narrower than the 12th, there are similar problems off the tee here, and the drive needs to find the grass between the bunkers at 260 yards and a chain of three farther up on the left. The main feature on the green is a 40-yard ridge running from front to back.

No 14 • 547 yards Par 5
The ultimate driving test with the wind off the left and out of bounds (Prince's Golf Club) to the right. Danger lurks everywhere and going for the green in two takes nerve. The Suez Canal crosses the fairway at 330 yards. The right side of the green falls towards out of bounds.

No 15 • 496 yards Par 4
One of the hardest holes on the course and now, with a new tee back right, the longest par 4 after the addition of 21 yards. Five bunkers pinch the driving zone, but it is the three bunkers in front of the green that must be avoided at all costs. The green falls away on both sides.

No 16 • 163 yards Par 3
Not quite as encircled with bunkers as it was, the one back right having been removed. But Thomas Bjorn's nemesis remains, halfway up the right side of the green from which the Dane took three to escape in 2003 to lose his lead. Scene of the first televised hole-in-one by Tony Jacklin in 1967.

No 17 • 426 yards Par 4
The fairway has been widened by six yards after three-quarters of the field found it impossible to hold in the 2003 Open. A false front to the green means any approach short of ideal will roll back down the fairway. Paul Lawrie holed his second shot here in 1993.

No 18 • 459 yards Par 4
The fairway has been moved to the right to provide a better landing zone, but more bunkers are now in play off the tee. Three cross bunkers have become two, but the bunker short left of the green has been moved in closer to the green. Duncan's Hollow on the left remains, however.

The 163-yard 16th was the scene of the first televised hole-in-one, by Tony Jacklin in the 1967 Dunlop Masters.

"prediction" did become fact. Six years later, in 1928, Hagen made the most diligent preparations before taking the title again. He went as far as "locking up my little black book" and refusing to give in to the "tempting phone calls."

Duncan's Hollow again played a part in 1985 when Lyle ended up there. Like Duncan, his first attempt to crest the bank and stay on the green failed. He tried again and made a bogey, but as it turned out, unlike for Duncan, it was ultimately irrelevant. His was the first victory by a home player since Tony Jacklin in 1969, who in turn was the first British Champion since Max Faulkner in 1951.

By 1934, Britain had endured the first great American domination of the sport for more than a decade. Having Cotton become the new British hero was the boost the game needed. Cotton knew how to cash in, making appearances at the London Palladium, but his opening two rounds of 67 and 65, the latter an Open record and the inspiration for Dunlop's famous ball, were astonishing. He led by nine strokes, and by 10 after the third round. The last round should have been a lap of honour but he faltered. A 79, however, still gave him a five-stroke victory. Taylor was present to witness Cotton's arrival as an Open Champion, but Vardon, who was unwell, was back at his hotel. Cotton went round to the hotel that night and placed the Claret Jug in the old master's hands.

With no home player having won The Open for more than a decade but with British players dominating the top of the World Ranking, the question was whether any of them could do a Cotton or a Lyle and become a new hero?

Exempt Competitors

Name, Country	Category	Name, Country	Category
Thomas Aiken, South Africa	9	Trevor Immelman, South Africa	13
Robert Allenby, Australia	6, 16	Ryo Ishikawa, Japan	25
Fredrik Andersson Hed, Sweden	7	Fredrik Jacobson, Sweden	18
Aaron Baddeley, Australia	17	Raphael Jacquelin, France	9
SM Bae, Korea	26	Thongchai Jaidee, Thailand	7
Ricky Barnes**, USA	6	Scott Jamieson, Scotland	11
Lucas Bjerregaard, Denmark	31	Miguel Angel Jimenez, Spain	6, 7, 20
Thomas Bjorn**, Denmark	6	Dustin Johnson, USA	6, 16, 20
Jonathan Byrd, USA	6	Zach Johnson, USA	6, 13, 16, 20
Angel Cabrera, Argentina	12, 13	Robert Karlsson, Sweden	6, 7
Mark Calcavecchia, USA	1	Hiroo Kawai, Japan	27
Paul Casey, England	5, 6, 7, 8, 16	Martin Kaymer, Germany	5, 6, 7, 14, 20
KJ Choi, Korea	6, 15, 16	Brad Kennedy, Australia	26
Stewart Cink, USA	1, 2, 4, 20	Simon Khan, England	7, 8
Darren Clarke, Northern Ireland	7	Anthony Kim, USA	6
Nicolas Colsaerts, Belgium	9	KT Kim, Korea	6, 24
Ben Crane, USA	6, 16	Matt Kuchar, USA	6, 16, 20
Ben Curtis, USA	1, 2, 4	Martin Laird, Scotland	6, 16
John Daly, USA	1	Bernhard Langer, Germany	28
Rhys Davies, Wales	7	Pablo Larrazabal, Spain	10
Jason Day, Australia	6, 16	Paul Lawrie, Scotland	1
Luke Donald, England	6, 7, 8, 16, 20	Tom Lehman, USA	1
Jason Dufner, USA	6	Justin Leonard, USA	1, 4
David Duval, USA	1, 2	Joost Luiten, Netherlands	7
Simon Dyson, England	6	Sandy Lyle, Scotland	1
Ernie Els, South Africa	1, 2, 4, 6, 7, 16	Bryden Macpherson, Australia	29
Ross Fisher, England	7, 20	Hunter Mahan, USA	6, 16, 20
Rickie Fowler, USA	6, 20	Matteo Manassero, Italy	6
Harrison Frazar, USA	18	Steve Marino, USA	6
Hiroyuki Fujita, Japan	25	Prayad Marksaeng, Thailand	26
Jim Furyk, USA	6, 16, 20	Graeme McDowell, Northern Ireland	6, 7, 12, 20
Stephen Gallacher, Scotland	7	Rory McIlroy, Northern Ireland	5, 6, 7, 12, 20
Sergio Garcia, Spain	10	Phil Mickelson, USA	6, 13, 16, 20
Robert Garrigus, USA	6	Edoardo Molinari, Italy	6, 7, 20
Lucas Glover, USA	12	Francesco Molinari, Italy	6, 7, 20
Retief Goosen, South Africa	5, 6, 7, 16	Ryan Moore, USA	6, 16
Richard Green, Australia	7	Kevin Na, USA	16
Bill Haas, USA	6	Seung-Yul Noh, Korea	21
Todd Hamilton, USA	1, 2	Geoff Ogilvy, Australia	6, 16, 22
Anders Hansen, Denmark	6, 7	Sean O'Hair, USA	5
Peter Hanson, Sweden	6, 7, 20	Thorbjorn Olesen, Denmark	11
Padraig Harrington, Republic of Ireland	1, 2, 4, 6, 7, 14, 20	Mark O'Meara, USA	1
Gregory Havret, France	7	Louis Oosthuizen, South Africa	1, 2, 5, 6, 7
Charley Hoffman, USA	16	Jeff Overton, USA	16, 20
JB Holmes, USA	6	Ryan Palmer, USA	6, 16
Charles Howell III, USA	19	Ian Poulter, England	6, 7, 20
Jung-Gon Hwang, Korea	26	Alvaro Quiros, Spain	6, 7
Yuta Ikeda, Japan	6	Robert Rock, England	5
		Justin Rose, England	6, 16

Name, Country	Category	Name, Country	Category
Rory Sabbatini, South Africa	6	Bo Van Pelt, USA	6, 16
Charl Schwartzel, South Africa	6, 7, 13, 23	Camilo Villegas, Colombia	16
Adam Scott, Australia	6, 16	Nick Watney, USA	5, 6, 16
Webb Simpson, USA	6	Bubba Watson, USA	6, 16, 20
Vijay Singh, Fiji	6	Tom Watson, USA	4
Brandt Snedeker, USA	6	Lee Westwood, England	5, 6, 7, 20
Kyle Stanley, USA	19	Danny Willett, England	7
Henrik Stenson, Sweden	5, 15	Mark Wilson, USA	17
Kevin Streelman, USA	16	Gary Woodland, USA	17
Steve Stricker, USA	6, 16, 20	YE Yang, Korea	6, 14
Tadahiro Takayama, Japan	27		
Peter Uihlein, USA	30		

* Denotes amateurs   **Denotes reserves

Key to Exemptions from Regional, Local Final and International Final Qualifying

Exemptions for 2011 were granted to the following:

(1) Past Open Champions aged 60 or under on 17 July 2011.

(2) The Open Champions for 2001-2010.

(3) Past Open Champions born between 17 July 1945 and 19 July 1948.

(4) Past Open Champions finishing in the first 10 and tying for 10th place in The Open Championship 2006-2010.

(5) First 10 and anyone tying for 10th place in the 2010 Open Championship at St Andrews.

(6) The first 50 players on the Official World Golf Ranking for Week 21, Monday 30 May 2011.

(7) First 30 in the Race to Dubai for 2010.

(8) The BMW PGA Championship winners for 2009-2011.

(9) First 3 and anyone tying for 3rd place, not otherwise exempt, in the top 20 of the Race to Dubai for 2011 on completion of the 2011 BMW PGA Championship.

(10) First 2 European Tour members and any European Tour members tying for 2nd place, not otherwise exempt, in a cumulative money list taken from the 6 official European Tour events leading up to and including the 2011 BMW International Open.

(11) The leading player, not otherwise exempt, in the first 5 and ties of each of the 2011 Open de France ALSTOM and the 2011 Barclays Scottish Open. With the exception of ties for first place, which will be determined in accordance with the Conditions for the tournament concerned, ties will be decided in favour of the highest Official World Golf Ranking player at the commencement of the tournament.

(12) The US Open Champions for 2007-2011.

(13) The US Masters Champions for 2007-2011.

(14) The US PGA Champions for 2006-2010.

(15) The PLAYERS Champions for 2009-2011.

(16) The leading 30 qualifiers for the 2010 TOUR CHAMPIONSHIP.

(17) First 3 and anyone tying for 3rd place, not exempt having applied (6) above, in the top 20 of the US PGA TOUR FedExCup Points List for 2011 on completion of the Crowne Plaza Invitational at Colonial.

(18) First 2 US PGA TOUR members and any US PGA TOUR members tying for 2nd place, not exempt, in a cumulative money list taken from the US PGA TOUR PLAYERS Championship and the five US PGA TOUR events leading up to and including the 2011 AT&T National.

(19) The leading player, not exempt having applied (18) above, in the first 5 and ties of each of the 2011 AT&T National and the 2011 John Deere Classic. With the exception of ties for first place, which will be determined in accordance with the Conditions for the tournament concerned, ties will be decided in favour of the highest Official World Golf Ranking player at the commencement of the tournament.

(20) Playing members of the 2010 Ryder Cup teams.

(21) First and anyone tying for 1st place on the Order of Merit of the Asian Tour for 2010.

(22) First and anyone tying for 1st place on the Order of Merit of the Tour of Australasia for 2010.

(23) First and anyone tying for 1st place on the Order of Merit of the Southern Africa PGA Sunshine Tour for 2010.

(24) The Japan Open Champion for 2010.

(25) First 2 and anyone tying for 2nd place, not exempt, on the Official Money List of the Japan Golf Tour for 2010.

(26) The leading 4 players, not exempt, in the 2011 Mizuno Open. With the exception of ties for first place, which will be determined in accordance with the Conditions for the tournament concerned, ties will be decided in favour of the highest Official World Golf Ranking player at the commencement of the tournament.

(27) First 2 and anyone tying for 2nd place, not exempt having applied (26) above, in a cumulative money list taken from all official 2011 Japan Golf Tour events up to and including the 2011 Mizuno Open.

(28) The Senior Open Champion for 2010.

(29) The Amateur Champion for 2011.

(30) The US Amateur Champion for 2010.

(31) The European Amateur Champion for 2010.
(29) to (31) were only applicable if the entrant concerned was still an amateur on 14 July 2011.

Local Final Qualifying
28 - 29 June

Littlestone

Andy Smith, England	70 68	138
Marcus Brier[P], Austria	69 70	139
Lee Corfield[P], England	70 69	139

Prince's

Simon Edwards, England	68 69	137
Thomas Shadbolt, England	66 73	139
Francis McGuirk, England	68 71	139

Royal Cinque Ports

Craig Hinton*, England	69 70	139
Andrew Johnston[P], England	66 74	140
Simon Lilly[P], England	70 70	140

Rye

Tom Lewis*, England	63 65	128
Adrian Wootton, England	63 68	131
Mark Laskey[P], England	65 68	133

* Denotes amateurs   [P]Qualified after playoff

1. Littlestone
2. Prince's
3. Royal Cinque Ports
4. Rye

London

ROYAL ST GEORGE'S

The Starting Field (from Entry Form)

"In the event of an exempt player withdrawing from the Championship or further places becoming available in the starting field after the close of entries, these places will be allocated in the ranking order of entrants from OWGR (Official World Golf Ranking) at the time that intimation of withdrawal is received or further places are made available by the Championship Committee. Any withdrawals following issue of OWGR Week 27 will be taken in ranking order from OWGR Week 27."

Thomas Bjorn, Denmark, replaced Vijay Singh, Fiji
Ricky Barnes, USA, replaced Nicolas Colsaerts, Belgium

Marcus Brier

Thomas Shadbolt

Andrew Johnston

Tom Lewis

International Final Qualifying

ASIA   24 & 25 February
Amata Spring   *Bangkok, Thailand*

Prom Meesawat, Thailand	67	65	132
Tetsuji Hiratsuka, Japan	70	64	134
Chih-Bing Lam, Singapore	68	67	135
Jason Knutzon, USA	69	67	136

Prom Meesawat

AMERICA   23 May
Gleneagles   *Plano, Texas*

Brian Davis, England	64
Chad Campbell, USA	65
Nathan Green, Australia	66
Davis Love III, USA	66
Spencer Levin, USA	66
Chris Tidland, USA	66
Bob Estes, USA	66
Jerry Kelly[(P)], USA	67

[(P)] Qualified after playoff
Due to adverse weather conditions (lightning), this competition was reduced to 18 holes.

Brian Davis

AUSTRALASIA   11 January
Kingston Heath   *Melbourne, Australia*

Matthew Millar, Australia	66	68	134
Kurt Barnes, Australia	66	69	135
Rick Kulacz[(P)], Australia	70	66	136

[(P)] Qualified after playoff

Matthew Millar

EUROPE

6 June

Sunningdale — *Berkshire, England*

Graeme Storm, England	65	62	127
Alexander Noren, Sweden	66	64	130
Gary Boyd, England	65	66	131
Thomas Levet, France	65	66	131
Peter Whiteford, Scotland	67	64	131
Alejandro Canizares, Spain	67	65	132
Kenneth Ferrie, England	68	64	132
Gregory Bourdy, France	67	65	132
Richard McEvoy, England	64	68	132
George Coetzee[P], South Africa	68	65	133

[P] Qualified after playoff

Graeme Storm

AFRICA

19 & 20 January

Royal Johannesburg & Kensington — *Johannesburg, South Africa*

Floris De Vries, Netherlands	64	68	132
Neil Schietekat, South Africa	70	66	136
Martin Maritz, South Africa	69	67	136

Floris De Vries

Royal St George's

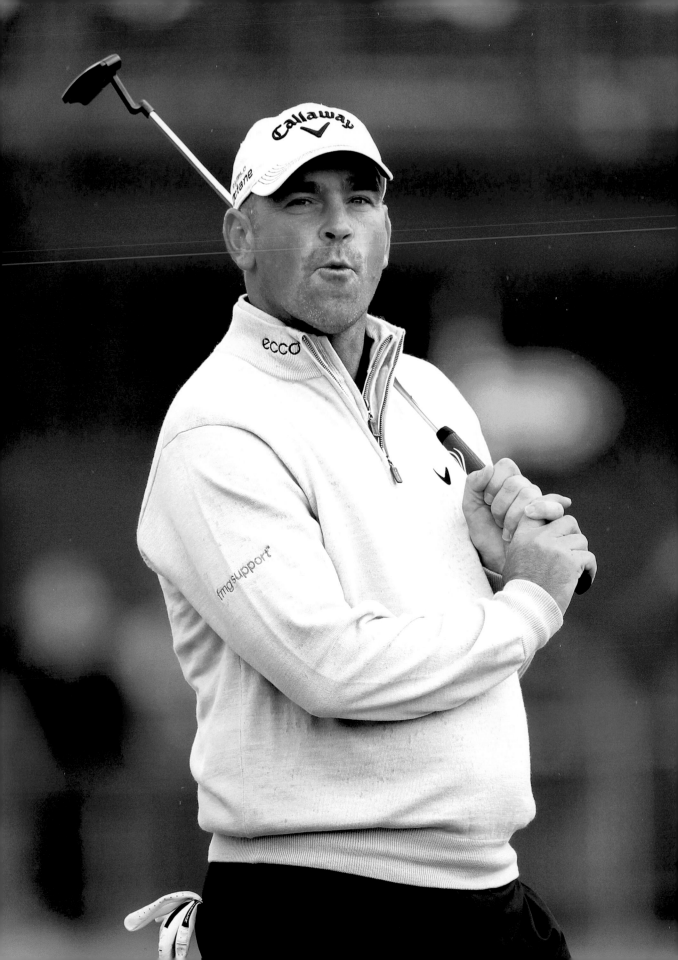

First Round

An Odd Couple Lead the Way

By Andy Farrell

Amateur Tom Lewis produces a record score to join Thomas Bjorn at the top of the leaderboard on the first day.

It is generally acknowledged that Royal St George's, with its humps and hollows, its blind and semi-blind shots, requires more knowing than most Championship courses. Perhaps that is why the leaderboard after the first round of the 140th Open Championship, with its pair of Toms at the top, ended up looking like an advert for a satellite navigational device. Thomas Bjorn and Tom Lewis led the way with five-under-par rounds of 65, one ahead of Miguel Angel Jimenez, Lucas Glover, and Webb Simpson.

Once more the Sandwich links, infuriating and intriguing in equal measure, proved its capacity to throw up surprises is enduring. The last time The Open swung by the Kent coast, Ben Curtis, then the world No 396, claimed the Claret Jug. Bjorn might have won that Open but for a late collapse

Thomas Bjorn's 65 came in a less-favourable early start time.

which made his return to the leaderboard now — as a late reserve and months after the death of his father — all the more poignant.

About the only link between Bjorn and Lewis was their sharing of the same coach, Peter Cowen. But of all his charges, including defending Champion Louis Oosthuizen and world number two Lee Westwood, not even Cowen might have guessed the identity of the two who sat at top of the pile. They made for an odd couple, Bjorn, experienced and emotional, Lewis a brilliant amateur whose record-breaking Championship debut upstaged an Open great. When Tom Watson hangs back at the 18th hole to allow another competitor the full embrace of a standing ovation, as ever generous he did for Lewis late on this Thursday evening, something of significance has surely happened.

"There were a lot of cheers for Tom today," Lewis said. "At first it was for Tom Watson and then towards the end when I was playing well, I think they were cheering for me as well. I was really grateful and I had a great time out there."

Lewis beat by one stroke the amateur record for The Open of 66 set by Frank Stranahan in 1950

1

Mowers were on the golf course before dawn, as seen at the 18th hole.

Jerry Kelly had the honour on the first tee.

and equalled by Tiger Woods in 1996 and Justin Rose in 1998. It was the first time that an amateur had topped the leaderboard in The Open since Sir Michael Bonallack shared the first-round lead with Brian Barnes in 1968.

With all the excitement about the home challenge at the 140th Open, the 20-year-old amateur, from Sir Nick Faldo's old club of Welwyn Garden City, was hardly given a thought amid the attention on US Open Champion Rory McIlroy, world number one Luke Donald, Westwood, and the rest. But one or two of the cognoscenti thought it worth keeping an eye on Lewis. After all, Cowen would be wasting his time unless he was a prospect with enormous potential. Cowen called Lewis the most professional amateur he had ever worked with, and the Walker Cup captain, Nigel Edwards, was also fulsome in his praise.

Unlike Bjorn and most of the professionals who had not been back since 2003, Lewis played in the

Tom Lewis (right) completed his 65 with a chip to four feet.

First Round Leaders

HOLE	1	2	3	4	5	6	7	8	9	10	11	12	13	14	15	16	17	18	TOTAL
PAR	4	4	3	4	4	3	5	4	4	4	3	4	4	5	4	3	4	4	TOTAL
Thomas Bjorn	4	(3)	3	4	4	3	(4)	(3)	[5]	4	3	(3)	4	(4)	(3)	(2)	4	[5]	65
Tom Lewis*	4	4	(2)	4	4	3	(4)	(3)	4	4	[4]	4	[5]	(4)	(3)	(2)	(3)	4	65
Miguel Angel Jimenez	4	4	3	(3)	4	3	5	4	(3)	4	3	(3)	4	5	4	3	(3)	4	66
Lucas Glover	4	[5]	3	4	4	3	5	4	(3)	(3)	3	4	4	5	4	(2)	(3)	(3)	66
Webb Simpson	4	4	3	4	4	3	5	4	4	(3)	3	(3)	4	5	4	3	(3)	(3)	66

*Denotes amateur

Excerpts
FROM THE Press

"The British summer has a new hero, a 20-year-old amateur with an electric-blue stare whose dash at golf's established order in the early evening pumped a thousand volts through The Open Championship."

—Kevin Garside, *The Daily Telegraph*

"People have been tiptoeing around Thomas Bjorn and his memories of Royal St George's for eight years now. How else to react in a mind game like golf when someone's mind betrays them so completely?"

**—Christopher Clarey,
*International Herald Tribune***

"As the course veered nearest the rocky levee separating Royal St George's and the whitecaps whipping around in the blustery English Channel, American Gary Woodland pointed a finger towards the sky and smiled. The heavens were grey, but the sun was trying mightily to break through…. 'Almost,' Woodland laughed."

—Steve Elling, CBS Sports.com*

"For three Australians the lure of another appetising occasion in the not-too-distant future is in the back of the mind. Robert Allenby, Geoff Ogilvy, and Aaron Baddeley have begun their Open campaigns just outside the automatic entry places for a berth in the Presidents Cup, to be held at Royal Melbourne in November."

—Chris Barrett, *The Age*

As the wind died, Lucas Glover posted a 66 with 31 on the inward nine.

Amateur Championship at Sandwich in 2007 and won the Boys Amateur Championship on the links in 2009. He returned having played a lot of links golf, all but one of his tournaments in 2011 having been at the seaside, and in top form having won the St Andrews Links Trophy the previous month. In Local Final Qualifying, he topped the leaderboard at Rye by three strokes with rounds of 63 and 65 at the par-69 links along the coast.

Then came the draw for The Open which saw Lewis placed alongside Henrik Stenson and Watson, for whom Lewis had been named. The five-time Champion was a hero of Lewis' father Bryan, a former Tour player, who also named Tom's younger brother Jack, in honour of Jack Nicklaus. Lewis introduced himself to Watson on the day before the Championship, and it also helped that on the first tee on Thursday Stenson walked up and made the "Tom Tom" joke. "At least I shouldn't get lost today," said the Swede.

Still, Lewis' only thought on the first tee was "not wanting to embarrass myself" in front of Watson. It helped that he holed from

Officials and fans alike paid tribute to the late Seve Ballesteros, three times The Open Champion.

10 feet for a par at the first, got up and down from off the second green, and then hit a 4-iron to 12 feet at the short third. He holed the putt for a birdie and that really settled his nerves. In fact, he single-putted the first eight greens, claiming two more birdies at the long seventh and the eighth, where he holed from 15 feet.

It had been a wet and windy morning, but now it was warming up and the wind was calming down. It was an advantage for the afternoon starters, but with two bogeys in three holes it looked as if Lewis' dream start might be wasted. He found a bunker at the short 11th and then drove into a bunker on the 13th. Yet from the 14th tee onwards, his round could not have gone better. He found the front of the 14th green in two and two-putted for his birdie-4. A 6-iron to eight feet at the 15th produced another birdie, as did a 7-iron to six feet at the short 16th. At the next he rolled in a 20-footer for a fourth birdie in a row and his name went to the top of the leaderboard.

"I felt like that putt was holeable," Lewis said. "I felt like I could get it to the hole no matter how softly I hit it. It was an excellent putt." Despite the

Webb Simpson's 66 featured birdies on the last two holes.

First Round Scores	
Players Under Par	35
Players At Par	15
Players Over Par	106

Louis Oosthuizen (left) started his Open defence with a 72, while Martin Kaymer, the 2010 PGA winner, posted a 68.

Simon Dyson was in the 68 group.

sort of reception at the last hole that Watson has enjoyed a time or two but was utterly new to Lewis, he got up and down, confidently holing out from four feet. "I was just thrilled to be here, but to shoot 65 in the first round was something I wouldn't have thought," Lewis said. "I was just glad to get the drive off the first tee."

It was an uplifting finale to a day that began miserably enough. Bjorn said The Open was the one tournament where he looked forward to a tee-time before 8am. "So when I saw 7.25 I was quite pleased, even if it is not the easiest to get up at that hour and get yourself ready when the body is a little bit stiff," he said. "We never know what the weather is going to do, but more often than not it's better in the morning than it is in the afternoon."

On this day, however, the opposite was true. Of the 17 scores of two under par or better, only three came from players teeing-off before midday. The weather had been changeable all week. On Sunday and Monday, the early practice rounds were played in warm sunshine and light winds. On Tuesday and Wednesday, the wind switched and howled off the Dover Straits, making the par-3 11th almost unreachable even with a driver. For Thursday, the wind direction

Jogging to see his shot to the fourth, Pablo Larrazabal posted a 68 with no bogeys.

shifted again so that the first hole played downwind. Jerry Kelly, the American who was the first player to tee-off, was far from the last to go over the green. He made a bogey, but this was six strokes better than the 11 he made on the first hole of the 2003 Open.

Eight years ago the rough had been frighteningly thick and Kelly took several hacks on both sides of the fairway before taking an unplayable and then holing a putt from 30 feet to save his 11. A dry spring, followed by June rains, left the rough nowhere as severe, but the course was almost exactly where The R&A wanted it. Good scoring was possible, and Danny Willett, who won the Amateur Championship at Royal St George's in 2007, posted the first sub-par

Wind and Rain Are His Friends

Miguel Angel Jimenez, aged 47, was in with a 66, saying: 'It doesn't matter what your age is.'

Miguel Angel Jimenez has never spoken the best of English. He uses winks and shrugs to get his message across and the way he plays his golf is much the same. His swing is not the most orthodox, but he can cajole the ball into doing what he wants.

Conditions were not the best on the first morning, but Jimenez sees wind and rain as old friends. Instead of fighting the elements, he works with them, with his morning 66 much the same work of art as Thomas Bjorn's 65. Indeed, the only shot to cause any upset was his drive at the 18th. It had sailed into the right rough and finished in a lie so bad as to preclude any chance of going for the green and making a fifth birdie. He hacked out short en route to what was still, in most eyes, a pretty good par.

Jimenez's pre-round stretches prior to a round are mandatory viewing and not least because he never removes his cigar from his mouth. Having arrived on the practice ground, he bends down from the waist, leaning on a club. He then swirls his knees round in a couple of circles before lifting up the toe of each foot with his club-face.

A couple of regular swings, followed by some waist-high swings are next on the agenda — and then it is time for his drum-major routine, with clubs serving as drum-sticks as he loosens up his wrists.

It was put to him at the end of the first round that players his age (47) were not expected to be in the mix. All the pre-tournament chat had been about the Lee Westwoods, the Luke Donalds, and the Rory McIlroys. There was the usual jumble of words, but the Jimenez philosophy came out loud and clear: "It doesn't matter what your age is to be a good sportsman. On a links, you can see all the years, any age can be around the leaderboard. Just experience, just timing, just patience is something that age gives to you, no?"

Jimenez appreciated the many tributes to Severiano Ballesteros around the course, though he, like most of his compatriots, felt that it was time to move on. "The tribute to Seve here is very nice because we miss him and he make so much for golf all through his life," he said, and added as gently as he could that the players could not be expected to go on saying the same things over and over. They needed to be looking forward rather than back.

The interview over, Jimenez set off to stock up on logoed 2011 Open shirts for his family, himself included. By all accounts, he bought enough to clothe half Spain. And after that, he was on his way back to the hotel where he would have a glass of his favourite Rioja with his dinner. As he would explain: "There is more to life than golfing the ball."

—Lewine Mair

Fredrik Andersson Hed posted a 68.

Kyle Stanley also returned a 68.

"For the first time in 11 months, Rory McIlroy walked off the 18th green in the early stages of a Major Championship and did not see his name atop the leaderboard. That's how good he has been at golf's biggest events."

—**Doug Ferguson**, *The Associated Press*

"He's named after the man he played with during the first round of The Open Championship, and it really doesn't get any better than that. Except it did."

—**Bob Harig, ESPN.com**

"Ireland's Northern Lights blazed on the ancient links at Royal St George's as Rory McIlroy's long-time mentor Darren Clarke and best mate in golf Graeme McDowell stole the US Open Champion's thunder at The Open."

—**Karl MacGinty**, *Irish Independent*

"Webb Simpson hasn't played much links golf — a trip to Northern Ireland as a member of the United States Walker Cup team in 2007 is about the extent of it — but he's already developed a fondness for it."

—**Ron Green Jr**, *The Charlotte Observer*

"Padraig Harrington would have preferred to talk post-round about his birdies, rather than his flat cap which — apparently — had become something of an internet sensation during his opening round.... As for the new look flat cap? The Dubliner wore it to raise awareness for 'male cancer.'"

—**Philip Reid**, *The Irish Times*

score playing alongside Kelly in the first group. Mark Calcavecchia, the 1999 Champion, also had a 69 in the next group, once again enjoying an early Open tee-time.

Four groups later, Bjorn returned his 65 and Simon Dyson a 68. Dyson was due to be on holiday in Spain but was one of the first reserves to gain a place in the Championship when David Toms withdrew the week before. It was only on Monday night that Bjorn got a place when Vijay Singh pulled out due to a back injury. Bjorn had travelled down from the Scottish Open when he was the first

Luke Donald arrived after a win, but returned a 71.

Graeme McDowell, returning a 68, came back in 31.

Low Scores	
Low First Nine	
Tom Lewis*	32
Fredrik Andersson Hed	32
Low Second Nine	
Lucas Glover	31
Webb Simpson	31
Graeme McDowell	31
Low Round	
Thomas Bjorn	65
Tom Lewis*	65
*Denotes amateur	

reserve, but he was reluctant to talk extensively about the events of 2003, when he led by three strokes on the 15th tee but dropped four strokes in three holes, taking three of get out of a bunker at the 16th.

Perhaps, some people mentioned to him, he might not want to be here at all? "This is The Open Championship," he said, "where else would you want to be?" Having not expected to be playing, the 40-year-old had "promised myself I would focus on every single shot and go after every single shot."

Bjorn birdied the second hole by making a 20-footer. It was the longest of his birdie putts since his approach play was superbly controlled. He hit a 6-iron to 10 feet at the eighth and an 8-iron to 12 feet at the 12th, but the undoubted highlight of his round was his 2 at the short 16th. Avoiding the bunker on the right that now cannot be mentioned without reference to his name, Bjorn hit a 9-iron to eight feet, although he had to smile when the ball only just cleared one of the bunkers at the front. "That was just a smile of knowing that things were going my way today," said the Dane.

With wife Brenda, Mark Calcavecchia returned to his favourite event.

Ryan Palmer had three bogeys and 68.

Jeff Overton's 68 had three birdies.

Round of the **Day**

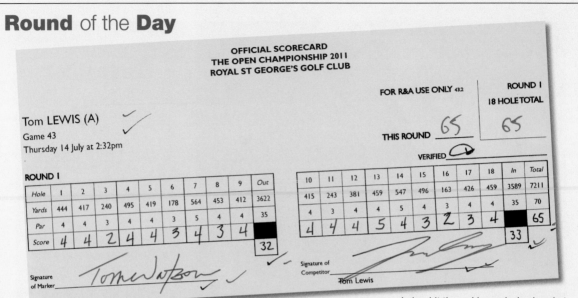

OFFICIAL SCORECARD
THE OPEN CHAMPIONSHIP 2011
ROYAL ST GEORGE'S GOLF CLUB

Tom LEWIS (A)
Game 43
Thursday 14 July at 2:32pm

FOR R&A USE ONLY 432 | ROUND 1 18 HOLE TOTAL

THIS ROUND __65__ | 65

VERIFIED

ROUND I

Hole	1	2	3	4	5	6	7	8	9	Out
Yards	444	417	240	495	419	178	564	453	412	3622
Par	4	4	3	4	4	3	5	4	4	35
Score	4	4	2	4	4	3	4	3	4	32

Hole	10	11	12	13	14	15	16	17	18	In	Total
Yards	415	243	381	459	547	496	163	426	459	3589	7211
Par	4	3	4	4	5	4	3	4	4	35	70
Score	4	4	4	5	4	3	2	3	4	33	65

Signature of Marker _Tom Watson_

Signature of Competitor _Tom Lewis_

For over 60 years the record had stood at 66 for the lowest individual round by an amateur. The American Frank Stranahan returned that score in 1950 in the final round at Royal Troon to share ninth place on 286. It wasn't until 1996 in the second round at Royal Lytham & St Annes that Tiger Woods equalled Stranahan's 66, and in 1998 in the second round at Royal Birkdale, Justin Rose also matched it.

Then, on the evening of the first round at Royal St George's, Tom Lewis came along with four successive birdies from the 14th hole to finish on 65 to break the amateur record and also take a share of the lead with Thomas Bjorn. He was the first amateur to lead The Open since 1968, when Sir Michael Bonallack was the leader with Brian Barnes on 70 at Carnoustie.

Lewis had eight putts in his first eight holes, hit three chips and a bunker shot within five feet, and was three under par. He dropped shots after hitting into bunkers at the 11th and 13th holes, then began his birdie run with two putts from the front edge on the par-5 14th. He hit a 6-iron to eight feet at the 15th, a 7-iron to six feet at the 16th, and an 8-iron to 20 feet at the 17th.

"To birdie from 14 onwards was something I didn't realise I was doing at the time," Lewis said.

Lewis had a late run with four birdies.

When he holed the putt, Bjorn had birdied four holes out of five and reached six under par. What would he have given for a 2, or a 3, instead of a 5 at the 16th in 2003? "Does that hole owe me anything? No. That hole owes nobody anything, no hole in golf does, no golf course does." He dropped a shot from Duncan's Hollow at the last but could not have been happier with his morning's work.

Bjorn was far from the only 40-something showing that experience was a great plus on a day like this. At 47, Jimenez was older than Old Tom Morris when he won the last of his four Open titles. "It doesn't matter what is your age to be a good sportsman," Jimenez said. "And this links, like all the years, any age can be around the leaderboard. Experience, timing, patience age gives you, no?" His

Steve Stricker posted a 69, coming to The Open after winning the John Deere Classic in America.

66 had the distinction of being the only morning round without a bogey, something matched later by Simpson and Pablo Larrazabal. They were, in fact, the only bogey-free rounds all week.

Much the most interest on the opening morning concerned the grouping of McIlroy, his fellow 22-year-old Rickie Fowler, and 2002 Champion Ernie Els. The new US Open Champion got a huge reception at the first tee but found himself alongside Fowler on the back fringe of the green, a long way from the hole at the front. Fowler went first and, remarkably, holed the putt. McIlroy hit a pretty good putt for length but far enough away to cause an opening three-putt bogey. Two holes later McIlroy missed the green at the third and went two over par. This was his first tournament

Ian Poulter birdied two of the last three holes for a 69.

Hitting his third shot to the 14th green, Rory McIlroy was happy with a 71, after bogeys on two of the first three holes.

Darren Clarke, with 68, joined the Irish challenge.

since the US Open, and after the poor start he was happy enough to get round in 71, helped by a birdie at the 17th. "It was nice to hang on," he said. His aim was to get back to at least level par after two rounds, which he figured would not be far away from the lead.

Fowler returned a 70 and Els a 72. The young American was alongside compatriot Dustin Johnson, who was feeling under the weather due to a throat infection and the fact he was four over through 12 holes. But he produced a moment of brilliance at the 163-yard 16th when he holed in one with a pitching wedge. He also birdied the 14th, 15th, and 17th holes before dropping a shot at the last. He was not exactly excited about his 70 afterwards, wanting to head home to rest, but he said: "Standing on the 14th tee I wanted to make some birdies and give myself a chance of getting back in this thing. If you would have bet me money that I would be

Round One Hole Summary

HOLE	PAR	YARDS	EAGLES	BIRDIES	PARS	BOGEYS	D.BOGEYS	HIGHER	RANK	AVERAGE
1	4	444	0	8	104	41	3	0	4	4.25
2	4	417	0	12	116	25	3	0	12	4.12
3	3	240	0	18	96	39	3	0	9	3.17
4	4	495	0	9	106	38	2	1	5	4.23
5	4	419	0	5	99	50	1	1	1	4.33
6	3	178	0	16	106	30	3	1	11	3.15
7	5	564	1	50	82	21	2	0	18	4.83
8	4	453	0	16	95	40	5	0	7	4.22
9	4	412	0	15	89	46	5	1	2	4.29
OUT	**35**	**3,622**	**1**	**149**	**893**	**330**	**27**	**4**		**36.58**
10	4	415	0	30	102	24	0	0	13	3.96
11	3	243	0	12	105	38	1	0	8	3.18
12	4	381	0	33	100	23	0	0	14	3.94
13	4	459	0	14	96	43	2	1	5	4.23
14	5	547	0	45	87	19	3	2	15	4.91
15	4	496	0	15	106	32	3	0	10	4.15
16	3	163	1	27	114	13	1	0	16	2.91
17	4	426	0	37	98	21	0	0	17	3.90
18	4	459	0	17	81	56	2	0	3	4.28
IN	**35**	**3,589**	**1**	**230**	**889**	**269**	**12**	**3**		**35.45**
TOTAL	**70**	**7,211**	**2**	**379**	**1,782**	**599**	**39**	**7**		**72.03**

Tom Watson posted a 72, his only birdie at the third.

Young Japanese star Ryo Ishikawa, who had a 74, was already four over when he saved par at the 16th from a bunker.

one under standing on the 18th tee, I would have taken it."

Ian Poulter, who was playing alongside Johnson, finished with two birdies in the last three holes to get back to one under. "I was joking with Dustin that neither of us were holing many putts, and then after his first birdie he laughed and said he got the lid off it," Poulter said. "We both finished with a few birdies after that."

Donald arrived in Kent after winning the Barclays Scottish Open at Castle Stuart the week before with a final round of 63. He seemed to be carrying on in the same mode when he birdied the third. His attempt for par at the sixth lipped out, which was an omen for the inward nine, but a 30-footer went in at pace on the seventh, so he turned one under.

Three bogeys in five holes, however, seemed to halt any momentum, and although he birdied the 17th, a 71 was not what he was looking for. It was the same score as McIlroy and also Westwood later in the day. Westwood seemed out of sorts after making three bogeys in a row from the third, and though his game was its usual consistent self from tee to green, he had 33 putts, too high to contend at championship level.

Glover, the 2009 US Open Champion, and Robert Karlsson had a chuckle on the 14th tee when they turned to each other and said: "Where did the wind go?" Both knew birdies could be more achievable and the bearded Glover finished with three in a row, holing from three feet at the 16th, two feet at the 17th, and 15 feet at the last. "It was a solid

Thomas Bjorn
Another Day, Going His Way

The 9-iron shot came down softly, some eight feet from the cup on the par-3 16th at Royal St George's, and Thomas Bjorn smiled the smile of someone as satisfied as he might have been relieved.

The demons had been vanquished. After eight years. "That," he would say, "was just a smile of knowing things were going my way."

Which were. Bjorn, at age 40 and in The Open as a reserve only because Vijay Singh had withdrawn, shared the first day's lead with the English amateur Tom Lewis.

Rare is the sporting event which takes place in a vacuum. Invariably there is a connection to earlier competition. For Bjorn, the connection was one the world wouldn't forget and he didn't want to remember.

Eight years earlier, 2003, at the same course, windswept Royal St George's, Bjorn led The Open by two shots with three holes to play. But at the fateful 16th he hit into a bunker.

Bjorn blasted onto the green, but short, and the ball trickled back into almost the original spot. His third shot stayed on the putting surface, and Bjorn took a double-

bogey-5, destroying his chances of winning a first Major.

In 2011, Bjorn, hardly the melancholy Dane, had been struggling in European Tour events preceding The Open. No one expected much from him, Bjorn included. "I don't, at the moment, play golf the way I used to do," he said. "But I did today."

Absolutely. Bjorn teed-off at 7.25am, made seven birdies, returned a 65, and came into the Media Centre trying to avoid discussing what happened in the previous Open, but of course was not able.

Bjorn's father, Olle, had died in May after a long illness, and his game had gone to pieces. When someone asked how proud Olle would have been of Thomas' elegant round, the emotions poured out.

"Well," said Bjorn, "he meant a lot to me." Then Bjorn choked up, stopped talking, and wiped his eyes. Memories flooded like tears.

"He would have been very proud of me. That's all I have to say."

That was enough. His clubs spoke eloquently, and for someone who didn't think he would be in the starting field, it was a round of reassurance.

"I never really expected to play," he said, "so there was no reason to get too uptight." No reason to dwell on what was.

"A lot of people have asked me what I feel about the 2003 Open," he conceded. "I mean it's in the past. People can write you off … but when you live in a career that's ahead of you, you try and make the best of every single day. And that's what I've done."

Bjorn, despite the failings of other days, came through this day.

"I've been very uncomfortable on the golf course for a long time," he said. "Today was one of those days where I saw the shots I needed to play and saw the golf course how I wanted to play it."

—Art Spander

round with some fireworks at the last," he said. His inward 31 was matched by Graeme McDowell and Simpson, who birdied the last two holes in his first appearance in The Open and only his second in a Major after finishing tied for 14th in the US Open. The 25-year-old American did, however, experience a classic links during the 2007 Walker Cup at Royal County Down.

McIlroy, Willett, and Rhys Davies played for Great Britain and Ireland in that match, while the winning American team contained not just Simpson but Fowler, Johnson, and Kyle Stanley, who scored a 68. Stanley, a 23-year-old from Gig Harbor, Washington, only got into The Open from the place on offer at the previous week's John Deere Classic, where he was runner-up to Steve Stricker. He had his passport with him ready to make the transatlantic trip, but he did need

Excerpts FROM THE Press

Padraig Harrington returned a 73 despite high Irish hopes.

to supplement his wardrobe for the conditions once over the pond.

However, Stanley was not the last man into the field, and nor was Bjorn. In fact it was Ricky Barnes, who had only an hour's notice before teeing-off, having flown over when first reserve and hearing that Nicolas Colsaerts had injured himself while falling off his scooter in Sandwich. Barnes kept up the high standard of those with late entries, matching Stanley's 68.

McDowell, the 2010 US Open Champion, also had a 68, which was a fine recovery after making a double-bogey from behind the first green. "My head was spinning," he admitted.

Darren Clarke, who helped celebrate both McDowell and McIlroy's US Open victories, also had a 68 after starting with a bogey at the first. He birdied the 10th to go one under, made his third bogey of the day at the 12th, but then birdied the 13th and 14th holes before parring in. "I didn't hole everything today by any stretch of the imagination, but I putted nicely," Clarke said.

"Any time I step back on a links I always enjoy it. This one is particularly difficult because of the undulations in the fairways and the demand that it puts on the second shots. It's just a tough, stern test. You've got to be patient this week, which has not always been one of my strong points. But that's what The Open is all about."

A NEW YOUNG TOM FOR THE OPEN

By Alistair Tait

Tom Lewis couldn't have asked for a better playing companion for his first Open Championship than five-time winner Tom Watson.

The 20-year-old English lad from Welwyn Garden City, Sir Nick Faldo's hometown, got a dream draw with his 61-year-old namesake as reward for getting into the Championship after topping the field in Local Final Qualifying at Rye.

Lewis isn't called Tom because parents Bryan and Lynda liked the sound of it. Bryan Lewis took preference when it came to naming their first-born son. "My dad was a golfer," Lewis said. "He played on the European Tour for a couple of years. Tom Watson was his hero, so I was the first son, so I was Tom."

Tom's younger brother Jack is named after Jack Nicklaus, so no prizes for guessing what career paths Bryan Lewis wanted his sons to follow.

Young Tom certainly has the talent to fulfil his father's wishes, but the prospect of playing with Watson had Lewis thinking more about preserving his dignity than trying to excel in the game's oldest Major.

"To play with Tom, no matter what I shot, was going to be excellent," Lewis said. "I was more (thinking of) not wanting to embarrass myself in front of him. I was just happy to get the drive off the tee on the first. That was all that mattered."

Lewis needn't have worried about his opening tee shot, or embarrassing himself. After eight holes it was obvious he wasn't going to crumble in front of the greatest links player of the modern era.

While Watson offset a birdie with a bogey over the opening eight holes, Lewis played that stretch in three under par. Bogeys at the 11th and 13th seemed to suggest Lewis had suddenly realised he was playing in The Open Championship, not his club championship. However, four consecutive birdies from the 14th to finish his round put him

into the record books with the lowest round ever by an amateur in The Open.

That birdie burst helped Lewis to a five-under-par 65 and into a tie for the lead with Thomas Bjorn. It marked the first time since Sir Michael Bonallack in 1968 that an amateur shared the first-round lead in The Open.

Mind you, Lewis had a little bit of home course advantage. Lewis won the 2009 Boys Amateur Championship over Royal St George's. He also warmed up for The Open with a victory in the St Andrews Links Trophy, one of the most prestigious titles in the amateur game.

"I play links courses all year, so I've had more advantage than anyone else in the field probably," Lewis said. "I've only played one (tournament) this year that's not been on links. So obviously I knew that if I did play well, which I was at the time, I could have shot a good score. But I didn't really have a target in my head."

Watson's own hopes of trying to get into contention to win his sixth Open were hampered by four bogeys. Two birdies helped minimize the damage. Yet two years after Watson lost a playoff to Stewart Cink at Turnberry, reporters weren't interested in his round. All the waiting press wanted to talk about was Young Tom.

"He's quite a refined player at age 20," Watson said of his young companion. "We certainly have a new young breed out here, don't we? We've got the McIlroys and the Ishikawas and the Lewises. We have a lot of young players playing very good golf. I just had to smile inside to watch him play. I didn't play particularly well myself, but I certainly was impressed by the way he played."

Good performances by amateurs in recent Opens are becoming more predictable. After all, Rory McIlroy made a similar impression in the 2007 Open at Carnoustie, when he returned a flawless opening-round 68. Meanwhile, Chris Wood finished fifth at Royal Birkdale in 2008 while still a member of the unpaid ranks. Watson knows why the amateurs are giving the seasoned pros a run for their money on the game's biggest stage.

"When you're 20 years old, you're a pretty seasoned player when you have the ability to play the type of competition that these kids have a chance to play in. One of the things they do, they play in a lot more competition than I ever did or ever wanted to. The collegiate golf, for instance, in the States, you play a lot of tournaments. My competition really was comprised of four or five tournaments a year. That was about it for me. These kids are playing a lot of competition."

And Watson's advice for his young namesake?

"I think the most important advice is, don't get too complicated in your life," Watson said. "You can get very complicated by adding a lot of people and a lot of things in your mind. Keeping it pretty simple, keeping the mind free of clutter is the most important thing. You don't need the clutter."

There was nothing complicated about Tom Lewis' opening round. He looked like he belonged up there with the world's elite.

Clarke and Glover Rise, Stars Fall

By Andy Farrell

Darren Clarke and Lucas Glover take the lead, but many of the world's best do not make the cut, including world number one and number two.

The surprise on Friday was not the identity of the co-leaders at the halfway stage of this Open Championship, but their score. On a day when summer returned, the sun shone, the breeze returned to its prevailing south-westerly direction and, at least in the morning, merely tickled the swings of the world's best players before blowing with more gusto as the day went on. At Royal St George's this was a day to enjoy and, with a forecast for wind and rain over the weekend, to take advantage.

Yet where the leading score after 18 holes was five under par, after 36 holes it had retreated to four under, on 136, the mark of Darren Clarke and Lucas Glover. Clarke has always loved links golf and after a returning to live in Northern Ireland

Lucas Glover posted a 70, finishing with eight pars.

had many practice rounds at Royal Portrush, out in all weathers, under his belt. Glover was the US Open Champion in 2009 and brought all that Major Championship experience. He also had a beard, prompting feverish speculation that the American could become the most hirsute Champion since the 19th century.

Thomas Bjorn, one of the overnight leaders, was in the group one stroke behind on 137 along with Chad Campbell, Martin Kaymer, and Miguel Angel Jimenez. It only took one morning of warmth for the course to firm up considerably, and combined with some challenging hole locations, it meant scoring was not as low as everyone was expecting. The best scores of the day were the 67s of Masters winner Charl Schwartzel, 1996 Open Champion Tom Lehman, and France's Raphael Jacquelin.

Clarke added a second successive 68, Glover had a 70 following his opening 66. Campbell scored a 68, Kaymer a 69, Jimenez a 71, and Bjorn a 72. Tom Lewis, the amateur who shared the lead with Bjorn after the first round, slipped to a 74, while his playing companion, Tom Watson, showed the kid how to do it with a 70 that included a hole-in-one

2

Excerpts
FROM THE Press

"In the sunlight shining on a brilliant new generation of golfers there was another kind of glow here yesterday. This was the kind you see in the embers of an old, glorious fire. It came from Tom Watson, the last great man of his times, who helped shepherd the latest of today's wunderkind, England's Tom Lewis, through his Major baptism."

—James Lawton, *The Independent*

"Imagination and creativity are Phil Mickelson's gifts. A perpetually positive attitude also is part of his DNA. He also has an insatiable thirst for a challenge. Combine these elements and you should have a perfect match between player and links golf, which demands a kind of creativity we aren't often asked to use in America."

—Mark Cannizzaro, *New York Post*

"Lucas Glover is in prime position to go where no man has gone since the 1880s — wearing a beard into the winner's circle at The Open Championship."

—Steve DiMeglio, *USA Today*

"Like a pair of ill-fitting trousers around Darren Clarke's waist, things are getting pretty tight as the 140th Open Championship reached its halfway stage at a baking Royal St George's. 'My manager has always said that I play better when I'm fat, so I've been trying to adhere to that theory,' chuckled Clarke."

—Nick Rodger, *The Herald*

Darren Clarke acknowledged his birdie on the 18th for his second 68.

Second Round Leaders

HOLE	1	2	3	4	5	6	7	8	9	10	11	12	13	14	15	16	17	18	TOTAL
PAR	4	4	3	4	4	3	5	4	4	4	3	4	4	5	4	3	4	4	TOTAL
Darren Clarke	4	4	(2)	[6]	4	3	(3)	(3)	4	[5]	3	(3)	(3)	[6]	4	[4]	4	(3)	68-136
Lucas Glover	4	(3)	3	[5]	4	3	(4)	4	4	[5]	3	4	4	5	4	3	4	4	70-136
Chad Campbell	4	[5]	3	4	4	3	(4)	4	4	4	3	4	(3)	5	4	(2)	(3)	[5]	68-137
Martin Kaymer	4	4	3	4	4	3	(4)	[5]	4	4	3	4	4	(4)	3	4	4		69-137
Thomas Bjorn	4	[5]	[4]	[5]	(3)	3	(4)	4	4	(3)	3	[5]	4	[6]	3	4	4		72-137
Miguel Angel Jimenez	4	[5]	3	[5]	4	(2)	(4)	4	4	[5]	3	(3)	4	5	[5]	3	4	4	71-137
Pablo Larrazabal	4	4	3	4	4	3	5	(3)	[5]	(3)	3	4	4	[6]	4	3	4	4	70-138
Charl Schwartzel	4	(3)	(2)	4	(3)	3	5	4	[5]	(3)	(2)	4	4	5	[5]	3	4	4	67-138
Davis Love III	4	4	(2)	4	4	(2)	5	4	4	4	3	4	[5]	(4)	4	[4]	4	(3)	68-138
Tom Lehman	4	(3)	3	4	4	3	(4)	[5]	4	4	3	(3)	4	(4)	4	3	4	4	67-138
George Coetzee	[5]	(3)	3	[5]	4	[4]	(4)	(3)	(3)	4	[4]	(3)	4	(4)	[5]	3	4	4	69-138
Dustin Johnson	4	4	3	4	(3)	3	(4)	[5]	(3)	4	3	4	4	5	4	3	4	4	68-138
Anders Hansen	4	(3)	3	4	[5]	3	(4)	4	4	4	[4]	(3)	4	(4)	4	3	[5]	4	69-138

at the short sixth. Lewis was still just under par, alongside the lurking Phil Mickelson, while Rory McIlroy, Rickie Fowler, and Sergio Garcia were at level par, just four behind. Watson was at two over, and 71 players at three over or better qualified for the weekend. They were covered by just seven strokes.

"The forecast for the weekend is very poor, which I quite look forward to," said Clarke. "The course is going to play very tough, so there's still two days of tough golf and tough weather ahead of us. The tournament is wide open for an awful lot of players."

Wide open certainly, but not to those who missed the cut, and the list of prominent names who failed to qualify was shocking. Two-time Champion Padraig Harrington and world number two Lee Westwood were among those on four over, only eight behind the leaders but going home. So were Justin Leonard, Ross Fisher, Danny Willett, and Hunter Mahan. At five over were Graeme McDowell, Nick Watney, Camilo Villegas, and Matteo Manassero. At six over were world number one Luke Donald, Robert Karlsson, Angel Cabrera, and John Daly. Had the 10-shot rule, long since abandoned, still

been in operation, exactly 100 players would have qualified for the weekend.

Still more did not make it: Ian Poulter, after rounds of 69 and 78, Geoff Ogilvy, Mark Calcavecchia, having gone 69-79, Bernhard Langer, Ernie Els, Ryo Ishikawa, and former Sandwich winners Sandy Lyle and Ben Curtis.

Westwood was bitterly disappointed not to be around for the weekend and was last seen heading for the car park. He and Harrington were placed 87th when they finished at lunchtime. Harrington said four over had "no chance of making it." At the end of the day they had worked their way up to a tie for 72nd, just two places away from making the cut. Westwood's frustrations can be viewed most clearly with reference to the official statistics which showed that no one had found more greens in regulation over the first two days but that only one player had taken more than his 68 putts — 33 on Thursday and 35 on Friday in his 73.

Harrington, who was wearing an old fashioned flat cap all the better to show off a badge for male cancer in support of a friend from the Wilson equipment company, bemoaned his putting as he had at St Andrews the year before. The Irishman

Martin Kaymer, sharing third place on 137, returned a 69 that he called 'very solid.'

Low Scores

Low First Nine

Stephan Gallacher	32
Nick Watney	32

Low Second Nine

Chad Campbell	33
Tom Lehman	33
YE Yang	33
Zach Johnson	33
Louis Oosthuizen	33
Gary Woodland	33

Low Round

Charl Schwartzel	67
Tom Lehman	67
Raphael Jacquelin	67

has the most curious record in The Open of late: He missed the cut in 2004, did not play in 2005 because of the death of his father, missed the cut in 2006, won both the next two years, was tied for 65th in 2009, and missed the cut in 2010 and 2011.

It would be enough to make anyone crazy, but it was actually McDowell, whose magnificent 2010 season included a US Open triumph and a starring role at the Ryder Cup, who said: "I'm a bit of a mental case out there right now."

McDowell opened with a 68 after a terrific inward nine but collapsed to a 77 without a single birdie on Friday. "Getting to be a habit, these types of days, and it's a bad habit to get into, obviously," he said. "I just can't string four rounds together at the minute, and this week, I couldn't even string two together."

The most worrying collapse of all was that of Donald, fresh from a confidence-boosting victory in the Barclays Scottish Open at Castle Stuart the week before. The week near Inverness had included many weather delays, but Donald said his energy levels had been fine. Nor

Thomas Bjorn battled to a 72 after starting with three bogeys in four holes.

Round of the Day

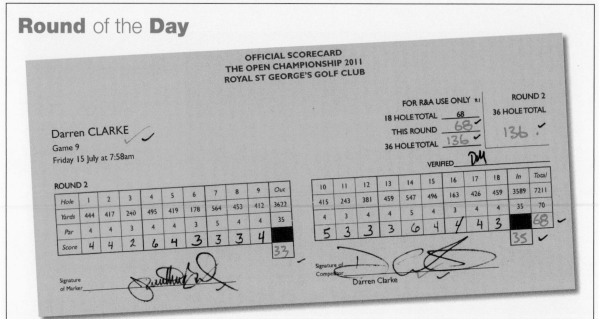

OFFICIAL SCORECARD
THE OPEN CHAMPIONSHIP 2011
ROYAL ST GEORGE'S GOLF CLUB

FOR R&A USE ONLY **9.1**   ROUND 2

18 HOLE TOTAL   68   36 HOLE TOTAL

THIS ROUND   68   136

36 HOLE TOTAL   136

VERIFIED   DM

Darren CLARKE
Game 9
Friday 15 July at 7:58am

ROUND 2

Hole	1	2	3	4	5	6	7	8	9	Out	10	11	12	13	14	15	16	17	18	In	Total
Yards	444	417	240	495	419	178	564	453	412	3622	415	243	381	459	547	496	163	426	459	3589	7211
Par	4	4	3	4	4	3	5	4	4	35	4	3	4	4	5	4	3	4	4	35	70
Score	4	4	2	6	4	3	3	3	4	33	5	3	3	3	6	4	4	4	3	35	68

Signature of Marker _____

Signature of Competitor _____ Darren Clarke

The shot which made Darren Clarke the most proud was "probably my little cut 7-iron into the last hole. I had to give myself a chance to make birdie after a couple of mistakes on 14 and 16." A very brave line for that shot? "Yes, I'm either very brave or very stupid," he said. "I don't know which one I am frequently. But it was a shot that I wanted to take on."

The shot from the rough on the right of the fairway finished 20 feet from the hole, then Clarke rolled home the birdie putt to finish with his second 68, two under par, and tied for the lead on 136 with Lucas Glover.

Clarke went out in 33, two under. He scored a birdie on the third hole with a 6-iron to 15 feet, but dropped two shots on the next hole when he drove into the rough and missed the green on his approach shot. Then his chip shot rolled back to his feet.

He got that back with an eagle-3 on the seventh, holing a 90-foot putt that hit the flagstick, and he also birdied the eighth. He scored three birdies and three bogeys on the inward nine.

The Northern Irishman said he benefited from having moved from London back home to Portrush. "It's a case of getting used to playing in bad weather on links again," Clarke said, "and that's what I've been doing all over the winter. Hopefully it will stand me in good stead."

Second Round Scores	
Players Under Par	22
Players At Par	22
Players Over Par	111

The shot which made Clarke's day — a 'little cut 7-iron' on the 18th hole.

Miguel Angel Jimenez said his four bogeys and three birdies for a 71 were 'not bad … in the conditions we played this afternoon.'

did he suggest the world number one tag had been a burdensome weight to be carrying. In fact, he could not offer an explanation for the four bogeys with which he finished, taking him from two over par and in with a chance of making a charge at the weekend, to six over and out of the Championship.

Dating back to the start of 1989, the period that the Official World Golf Ranking has retained computerised records, never before has the world number one and number two missed the cut in a Major Championship. "I probably got on the wrong side of the draw, but some other guys have dealt with it better than I have," Donald said. "It is very disappointing. I believe in my ability, but for whatever reason it has not happened in the last two Majors. I will continue to prepare as best I can."

Chad Campbell was drawing on his first Open in 2003.

Tom Watson and the crowd celebrated his hole-in-one on the sixth with a 4-iron shot that bounced once and jumped into the hole.

George Coetzee returned two 69s.

There was no doubting the players who played late-early had the better of the conditions, but that was no consolation to Westwood, nor indeed to Lewis. By the time the 20-year-old had finished all his media commitments after the first round and driven back to his hotel in Canterbury, it was time for bed and an early alarm call — multiple alarm clocks were set. Back out on the course at 9.30, the magic had gone. He drove into a bunker at the fourth for a bogey and also dropped a shot at the sixth.

It was understandable given the hullabaloo surrounding Watson. The five-time Champion hit a 4-iron that bounced once and then jumped into the hole. It was his 15th hole-in-one ever but his first in The Open. He was just happy not to have to putt — three three-putts the rest of the way were the difference between a great moment and a great round that would have left the 61-year-old under par.

Down the long seventh, Watson and Lewis got chatting and the youngster, as annoyed at his score by the end as any professional would have been, was wise enough to realise that moment, with Watson passing on his "tips on how he's won and the courses he's enjoyed," was not just the best bit of the week but "definitely the highlight of my career so far."

In the Limelight Again
Watson Recalls His First Hole-in-One

On Friday, it was almost as if Tom Watson said to himself on the first tee: "Tom Lewis was very good yesterday. My hat's off to him. I enjoyed watching him. That 65 was a very good score. But now he is going to have to watch me." And with that Watson craftily put together a round of 70, four strokes lower than Lewis, and decorated it with a 1 on the sixth hole.

It was Watson's 15th hole-in-one of his career, and the fact that it was hit with a 4-iron on a hole measuring about 170 yards gives you an idea of both his accuracy and how the passing years have reduced his length. Lewis, by contrast, played a 6-iron, and some in the field played an even shorter iron.

"How ironic," Watson said. "I was watching Padraig Harrington and Colin Montgomerie discussing Open venues and what do they show? Gene Sarazen on the Postage Stamp (the eighth at Royal Troon) making a hole-in-one with a 5-iron. He hit a heck of a shot there. Beautiful swing. Maybe that's what

inspired me today."

It was Watson's second hole-in-one in a Major Championship. The first had been in the US Open at Baltusrol in 1980 on the fourth hole in the first round.

Just as clear in his mind was his first-ever ace. "Now that's a good story," Watson said enthusiastically. "When I was a lad of 11 or 12 I was playing by myself at the Kansas City Country Club and made a hole-in-one. I had read in *Golf Digest* that if you made a hole-in-one with a Dunlop ball you sent it in, it was connected to a plaque and they sent it back to you. So I went to the pro shop and told John Cosnotti, the assistant pro.

"John looked at the advertisement and said, 'Tom we've got a problem. You have to have a witness.' My elation went from up there to down here.

"Then John walked over to the window, looked 400 yards to the second hole, and said: 'You know, Tom, I saw that go in.' He put his signature on the scorecard and I still have that plaque with the Dunlop No 4 ball on it."

At that Watson's freckled face beamed, the smile that we know so well from seeing him hoist the Open trophy on five occasions. That smile has become as much a part of July as the event itself.

—**John Hopkins**

Lewis was still at one under par and would be playing with Mickelson on Saturday. The left-hander had quietly compiled scores of 70 and 69. "It's fun to be in contention heading into the weekend," he said. Keeping the ball low has always been a challenge for Mickelson, but this year he was doing it about as well as in 2004 when he was third at Troon.

With Lewis falling out of the lead, Bjorn found himself alone at the top of the leaderboard when he teed-off at 12.26. Three bogeys in a row from the second, having driven into bunkers at two of those holes, soon changed that. Simon Dyson, playing with Bjorn, birdied the first three holes and took the lead at five under but then bogeyed the fourth.

Davis Love III, the 2012 US Ryder Cup captain, returned a 68.

With one of Friday's three 67s, Charl Schwartzel advanced into the top 10 on 138.

Tom Lehman's 67 also placed him on 138.

With six holes to play the Yorkshireman was still in a share of the lead, but he dropped four shots, including a double-bogey at the 17th, to finish at level par.

Bjorn, rallying strongly in defiance of his recent form, got back to five under with a birdie at the 10th but dropped two shots on the back nine to finish one off the lead. "It wasn't the prettiest of days golf-wise," said the Dane, "but I'll take where I stand in the Championship right now. It's a great position, but everybody's that's there for the weekend can win it."

Asked if anyone might have an advantage in the sort of turbulent weather expected over the weekend, Bjorn answered: "Guys that have grown up with links golf. I mean, Darren (Clarke) is sitting right there at the top of the leaderboard, he's grown up at Portrush, he knows links golf well. Guys like that are used to playing in those conditions, used to practising in those conditions when they were younger, they obviously should have an advantage.

Raphael Jacquelin had a 67 to follow an opening 74.

But it's all about playing great. It's not about what you've done 20 or 30 years ago, it's about how you play the next two days."

Since Clarke returned to live in Northern Ireland, while at home he might play three times a week with friends at Portrush, regardless of the weather. "If it was bad in the winter we might have a couple of pints before," he said, "and several more afterwards."

This was almost the first occasion that Clarke was featuring prominently since the 2006 Ryder Cup at The K Club, where he performed heroically just weeks after the death of his wife Heather. Now engaged to Alison Campbell and with his sons, Tyrone and Conor, settled in Northern Ireland, Clarke had the chance to work on his golf game. But after a poor weekend in Morocco in April, when he went from just off the lead to finishing almost last, his manager Andrew "Chubby" Chandler packed him off on holiday. "I have never seen

Lee Westwood returned a 73 and missed the cut after a double-bogey on the eighth and four bogeys.

Donald, Westwood Out of Kilter

It seemed written in the stars that Englishmen would feature prominently in the 140th Open Championship. Alas, the stars were out of kilter.

Luke Donald and Lee Westwood entered The Open as the world number one and number two golfers respectively. Not surprisingly, they were heavy favourites in betting establishments in Deal and Sandwich. They were 12-1 second favourites behind Rory McIlroy at 8-1.

Both seemed good choices to become the first Englishman to win The Open since Sir Nick Faldo in 1992. That was especially true of Westwood, considering victory was the next sequential instalment in a run that went third in 2009 and second in 2010.

Westwood seemed well set after an opening 71, a score that could easily have been much better. "On the greens I didn't capitalize," he said. "What I thought were a few good putts didn't go

in. There were three or four that I thought I made a foot short or two foot short that turned away, and that's the difference between a 71 and a 67."

The Englishman spent time on the practice putting green after the first round to try to iron out the problem. It was wasted time. Westwood returned a second-round 73 that included three birdies alongside four bogeys and a double-bogey. He missed the weekend by a shot, his first missed cut in The Open since 2005.

Westwood used his putter 68 times in the first two rounds, second worst of the 155 players to finish 36 holes.

Donald fared better on the greens, but the rest of his game was nowhere near the standard that won him the Barclays Scottish Open the week before. That much was obvious over Royal St George's closing stretch. Donald bogeyed the last four holes in a second-round 75 that saw him miss the cut by three strokes.

"I know I have the ability to win a Major,"

Donald said. "I've got to figure out a better way to play The Open."

He's not alone.

Three other top-10 players missed the cut — Matt Kuchar (number seven), Graeme McDowell (number nine), and Nick Watney (number 10). McDowell looked like he would be in the mix come Sunday with an opening 68. However, a second-round 77 saw him miss the cut by two shots. As candid as ever, G-Mac wasted no time in assessing the reason: "My attitude has been pretty average the last two days, I'd have to say. Just not having a lot of belief in myself. I'm a bit of a mental case," he said.

He wasn't the only one leaving Sandwich feeling frustrated. Ian Poulter parlayed an opening 69 into a second-round 77 to head home. Indeed, 21 of the world's top 50 missed the cut. World No 24 Ernie Els, the 2002 Champion, missed his second consecutive cut after making 18 in a row between 1992 and 2009.

—**Alistair Tait**

Luke Donald bogeyed the last four holes for a 75 to miss the cut by three strokes.

Round Two Hole Summary

HOLE	PAR	YARDS	EAGLES	BIRDIES	PARS	BOGEYS	D.BOGEYS	HIGHER	RANK	AVERAGE
1	4	444	0	12	102	38	3	0	10	4.21
2	4	417	0	22	103	28	2	0	13	4.06
3	3	240	0	13	103	36	3	0	11	3.19
4	4	495	0	5	69	66	12	3	1	4.61
5	4	419	0	27	108	19	0	1	16	3.97
6	3	178	1	14	101	32	4	3	9	3.22
7	5	564	9	84	53	9	0	0	18	4.40
8	4	453	0	9	83	51	11	1	2	4.43
9	4	412	0	11	104	36	3	1	8	4.22
OUT	**35**	**3,622**	**10**	**197**	**826**	**315**	**38**	**9**		**36.32**
10	4	415	0	14	90	46	5	0	7	4.27
11	3	243	0	10	86	53	6	0	3	3.35
12	4	381	0	30	101	20	4	0	15	3.99
13	4	459	0	30	105	18	2	0	17	3.95
14	5	547	1	37	85	19	10	3	14	5.06
15	4	496	0	10	94	47	4	0	6	4.29
16	3	163	0	13	112	27	3	0	12	3.13
17	4	426	0	8	93	51	3	0	4	4.32
18	4	459	0	10	95	43	7	0	5	4.30
IN	**35**	**3,589**	**1**	**162**	**861**	**324**	**44**	**3**		**36.66**
TOTAL	**70**	**7,211**	**11**	**359**	**1,687**	**639**	**82**	**12**		**72.97**

Playing from behind the 18th green, Tom Lewis had a 74 with bogeys on the last two holes.

Dustin Johnson's 68 featured all pars on the last nine.

him so low with his golf," Chandler said, although Clarke denied that he actually wanted to quit the game at that time. Three weeks in the Bahamas did the trick and on his return Clarke picked up with a sports psychologist of old acquaintance, Mike Finnegan.

In early May Clarke won his next tournament, the Iberdrola Open in Mallorca, a vital reminder that when in contention he still knew what to do. On the flight home, on one of those airlines where the refreshments are not complimentary, Clarke paid the bill for every passenger. Only the fact that Clarke was playing in Mallorca rather than at The Players Championship, and not by choice, showed how far he had slipped down the pecking order.

Success for McIlroy at the US Open, and for other members of Chandler's ISM stable in recent times, perhaps played its part. At the Holywood celebrations for McIlroy, Clarke admitted, a few had turned to him and told him to "get my finger out." What better place than a quirky old links on the Kent coast, especially after being allocated Greg Norman's locker from 1993. The only issue was his putting, but early in the week he bumped into Dr Bob Rotella, the psychologist who had not worked with Clarke for 18 months. Clarke told Rotella that he felt he needed to hit every approach to a foot to have any chance of holing the putt. Rotella told Clarke to "go unconscious,"

Excerpts
FROM THE Press

"What a tossed salad this leaderboard has become as the 140th Open Championship makes the turn: Old-school guys … the cigar crowd … new-age kids … two-hanky comeback stories … unknowns … two amateurs … reps of a dozen countries packed into a handful of shots and all of them about to get soaked and/or blown around."

—Dave Perkins, *Toronto Star*

"The cream of British golf trudged away from Royal St George's last night as Luke Donald, Lee Westwood, Graeme McDowell, and Ian Poulter all missed the halfway cut on the Kent coast."

—Ian Ladyman, *Daily Mail*

"Simon Dyson believes he can still clean up at The Open despite sliding down the leaderboard. The Englishman birdied the first three holes to climb to five under after an opening 68. But he came crashing down to end up level after a poor finish."

—James Nursey, *Daily Mirror*

"Robert Allenby and Davis Love III were in the group behind on a sun-soaked English Friday morning when Tom Watson sent a 4-iron high into the cloudless sky on the par-3 sixth at Royal St George's. They didn't see the ball as it flew at the flag, but they didn't need eyes to know what had happened. Their ears told them that the old man by the sea had reeled himself in an ace."

—Robert Lusetich, FOX Sports

Phil Mickelson had a 69 to be three shots off the lead.

to think less about his putting stroke rather than more and treat it like any other daily activity that we all do every day without thinking.

At the second hole on Friday Clarke holed a birdie putt from 15 feet. A double-bogey at the fourth, where a chip down in the dell around the green returned to his feet, might have destroyed his momentum in the past. Not this week. At the seventh he holed a 90-footer from off the green that hit the flagstick and went in for an eagle. Another birdie followed at the eighth, while the back nine was a mixture of three bogeys and three birdies, the most important coming at the last with a beautiful "cut 7-iron" to 20 feet. The putt was swished in as if it was a Sunday finish. "It was a little bit more adventurous today than yesterday," Clarke said. "There was some good and some not so good, but overall a 68 is very pleasing."

While Clarke revealed he was due to go on Weight Watchers the following week, Glover was staying with Davis Love III, the 2012 Ryder Cup captain, and off the course their main leisure activity was "eating as much as we can." Two years after his Major breakthrough, Glover returned to the winner's enclosure at the Wells Fargo Championship in May. After a bogey at the 10th, he parred in for his 70 and joined Clarke in the clubhouse on 136. "I hit it better today than I did yesterday but didn't make as many putts," Glover said. "You have to put those two together to win big tournaments like this. I'm just glad I made the cut and I played well and I've got the afternoon off."

Love joined Clarke, Bjorn, and Jimenez in the 40-something brigade on the leaderboard with a 68 to be two under alongside Schwartzel, Lehman, and Dustin Johnson. Like Love, Johnson added a 68 to his opening 70. From four over after 13 holes, his position, like his health, was only improving.

In their private duel over the first 36 holes, McIlroy and Fowler finished on the same level-par score. After a 71 on Thursday, it was where

Padraig Harrington posted 71 with bogeys on the 10th and 14th.

Amateur Bryden Macpherson went out.

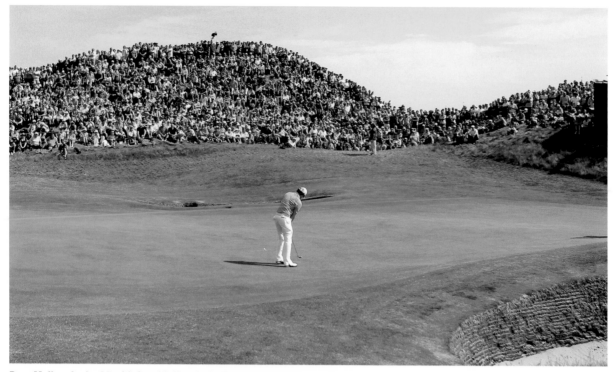

Rory McIlroy had a 69 with four birdies, including this at the sixth hole.

McIlroy wanted to get back to, and a 69 did the trick, while Fowler had a second consecutive 70. Twice McIlroy had two birdies in a row, but each time he bogeyed the next hole, so it was never quite full steam ahead. "Even though it was nice and sunny, it was very tricky," he said. "The course is playing a lot firmer, there are a lot of cross-winds, and to shoot something in the 60s today, I'm very pleased."

McIlroy, who was in the early-late half of the draw, added: "I was sort of bemoaning my draw early on this morning. I saw the guys finish up last night and it was flat calm, then this morning the sun was shining for them. But you can't do anything about it. You can only do the best you can and that's what I've tried to do the first two days.

"I'm happy with my position and if I get off to a decent start tomorrow I'm right in it." With reference to his compatriot at the top of the leaderboard, McIlroy said: "Yes, brilliant. This sort of golf really suits his game. He's grown up on links and he likes to play different shots. It's the sort of week where you've got to manage your game and he's good at that, changing the trajectory. It's good to see him up there. He's doing a bit better than me at the moment, but I'm planning on changing that."

IRISH SUCCESS DEFIES THE ODDS

By Lewine Mair

By the end of The Open, statistics would suggest that a man from Northern Ireland, population 1.7 million, is more likely to win a Major than the lottery, where the chances of a top prize are one in 14 million. In contrast to the lottery, winning The Open is not down to luck, though there is plenty to suggest that it can be catching.

In Ireland, where players from the North and South are one for the sake of international competition, the process started with Padraig Harrington when he captured two Open Championships and a PGA Championship across 2007 and 2008.

Harrington predicted at the time that there would be a knock-on effect, that we would see others following suit. He said then: "People who have known me all my life and have seen me on bad days as well as good will all be saying to themselves, 'If he can do it…'"

Graeme McDowell was one of them and he duly paid tribute to Harrington when he won the US Open at Pebble Beach in 2010. Then came McDowell's young friend Rory McIlroy, who in turn paid tribute to McDowell as well as Harrington.

Darren Clarke was among those who joined in the celebrations when McIlroy returned home after winning the 2011 US Open in June. Clarke had been mentoring McIlroy for years and was dripping with pride at what the young man had achieved. Other party-goers struck a chord when they suggested that it was time Clarke won a Major for himself.

Chubby Chandler, Clarke's manager of 21 years, was another to say that Clarke's time had come. Chandler had been put on the spot by a journalist who asked which of his key players of the moment, Lee Westwood or McIlroy, was the more likely to make off with the Claret Jug.

Not wanting to name Lee in front of Rory, or Rory in front of Lee, Chandler had exclaimed: "It might be Darren." As suggestions go, it was light-hearted but by no means laughable. After all, Clarke had shown form in winning in Mallorca earlier in the year.

Clarke's links game was as polished as it had ever been going into Open week.

With his wife Heather having died from breast cancer in 2006, Clarke decided that it would be better if he were to take his two sons, Tyrone and Conor, from England back to his homeland. That way, they would be among family members when he was away playing golf.

He waited until the moment was right and went ahead with the move in 2010.

In helping his boys, Clarke helped himself. After years of practising in relatively balmy conditions, he returned to the wind-tossed links of Portrush. "It was a case of getting used to playing in bad weather again," he explained after his 68 Friday at Royal St George's. "It's what I was doing all last winter and hopefully it will stand me in good stead."

You do not get to the top of the leaderboard at the halfway stage of an Open without thinking of what the next two days might bring. Great mood though he was in, Clarke was by no means oblivious to the mounting pressure.

Yet the week thus far had nothing on what he had gone through at the 2006 Ryder Cup at The K Club. That was when he was playing amid the grief of having just lost his wife.

"Nothing could be more difficult than that particular week," he said.

When McIlroy added a 69 to his opening 71, he was thinking less of being four shots off the lead than four behind Clarke. Said the Holywood golfer: "He's doing better than me at the moment, but I'm planning on changing that."

As for McDowell, he had matched Clarke's opening 68 but followed up with a disaster of a 77 to miss the cut. "I haven't been able to string four good rounds together in a while and this week I couldn't even string two together," he said.

McDowell had played beautifully in practice but not for too much longer. "By the time I walked off the first green on Thursday, I felt that I wasn't ready any more," he sighed. "It's all very frustrating."

But amid the disappointment, McDowell rejoiced in the way things were going for Clarke. "He's a great links player and he's the type of player who can still win tournaments, like he showed in Mallorca," McDowell said.

Asked what it would mean were Clarke to be the man lifting the Claret Jug, McDowell suggested that golfers all over the world would be relocating to Northern Ireland.

"The odds against us having three Major winners are pretty massive," McDowell said, "but it is amazing the way certain guys doing it can spur others on to do the same."

Third Round

Clarke Kicks Up a Storm

By Andy Farrell

A day of turbulent weather sees the Northern Irishman produce one of the greatest displays of ball-striking ever on these links.

On a Royal St George's day which would have had Henry Longhurst leaping out of bed as he did for the stormy conclusion of the 1938 Open but was a far less enticing prospect for the majority of those still playing in the 2011 Open Championship, Darren Clarke ended up playing the part of Reg Whitcombe. The Claret Jug could not be claimed after this third round, but it was Clarke who went to bed to sleep on the lead. The Northern Irishman was a stroke ahead of Dustin Johnson and three ahead of Thomas Bjorn and Rickie Fowler on a day that brought comparisons with the final day 73 years ago, albeit the tented village did not end up in Pegwell Bay.

Clarke and the overnight leaders actually got the best, or the least worst, of the conditions, but the authority with which the 42-year-old Clarke

Darren Clarke's 69 was one of three scores under par.

bestrode the links suggested a natural successor to Whitcombe. From the start of the round when in teeming rain he claimed the only birdie of the day at the first hole, to the finale at the 18th where his 25-footer came up just short for what would have been the only birdie of the day at the home hole, Clarke produced one of the greatest displays of ball-striking seen on this mighty links.

Were popular acclamation being taken into account, the result would not be in doubt. At least by the time he reached the 18th the umbrellas had come down and the gloves were no longer needed and the applause and roars were resounding. "The support given me this week has been incredible," Clarke said. "It's been wonderful and everyone was brilliant today. Even when I was giving myself opportunities and missing them, they were still roaring at me, 'Come on, Darren' and 'Come on, Dazza.' There's very few other tournaments where I would get that support, and it has been wonderful to receive it from the fans today. It's been absolutely brilliant."

Clarke had scored a 69 to top the leaderboard on 205, five under par. The only other scores under

Three over par after six holes, Phil Mickelson steadied himself for a 71 to be five shots behind.

par were the 68s of Johnson and Fowler. Bjorn had a 71 and was on two under with Fowler. The only other men left under par were Miguel Angel Jimenez, who had a 72, and Lucas Glover, who scored a 73.

Glover had been playing with Clarke and the pair kept up an animated conversation all the way around the course. Rarely, perhaps never, had Clarke seemed so relaxed on one of golf's biggest stages. This despite his round being far from flawless. "I couldn't hit the ball better from tee to green," he said. "That was about as good as I could do. On the green, it was not quite the same, to say the least, but from tee to green I was very pleased with the way I played."

After holing from 12 feet at the first, Clarke hit his approach at the second to three feet but missed. Other chances went a-begging, and he

Dustin Johnson (left) came in with 33 for his 68.

Out in 37, Miguel Angel Jimenez posted a 72.

Soaked to the Skin

The usual Open buzz was drowned out by the angry squalls on Saturday morning. The Open crowd is a tough one and the spectators poured in just the same, but they, no less than the players, had to go in for plenty in the way of course management. Not only were conditions slippery underfoot but the wind dictated where they stood. They were torn from some of the better vantage points, with the dunes at the third hole a case in point.

Australia's Matthew Millar, playing with a marker and round in 80, was the first of the golfers to set off into the storm. "I don't usually mind if the conditions are a bit tough, but they really got hold of me today," said the Australian, who had three other players in the 80-and-over bracket with whom to commiserate. "It didn't matter whether it was into the wind or down wind, it was really tough to keep dry."

Ryan Moore was soaked to the skin. "Everything was wet," said the exasperated American at the end of his 76. "I had eight towels in my bag."

Bo Van Pelt, the owner of an entirely respectable 73, was laughingly recalling the words of a friend who had been put out when he could not accompany Van Pelt to Royal St George's. "He said to me, 'I hope you get soaked and shredded by the wind,'" said Van Pelt. "He's back in Indiana and probably laughing at me right now."

Darren Clarke would have been able to negotiate all that weather, but that linksland equivalent of an old sea-dog did not start out until the worst of the storm was done. In the event, it was left to an American, the 61-year-old Tom Watson, to show everyone how to cope.

The best club in Watson's bag was his smile. Though there were times when the water was running down the old Champion's face and the wind was similarly on the attack, he never stopped embracing the conditions. "You just try to keep the grips dry, keep your wits about you," he said.

Watson also knew how to deflate the rampant gusts. "One of the things players of my generation learned is an old saying, 'Swing with ease into the breeze.' A lot of times, you can see these young kids out there trying to hit it really hard into the wind and that doesn't flight the ball very well. You know, hitting low stingers, things like that, you don't have to hit that hard. You can just flight it by swinging a little bit more easily and that will take the height off the ball."

For young golfers everywhere, Watson had delivered one of the finest lessons to come out of the 2011 Open.

—**Lewine Mair**

Dressed for the British summer, along with his fans, Sergio Garcia came in with a 74, four over.

Tom Watson seemed to enjoy his round in the rain with Ricky Barnes.

three-putted the fifth for a bogey and missed from 10 feet for his par at the eighth. "I hit some really poor putts and there were a few misreads, but I did the best I could on each one," Clarke said. Over the years he has not always been able to put up with such frustrations, but his now daily sessions with Dr Bob Rotella, the sports psychologist he bumped into earlier in the week, seemed to be helping. "I've seen him like this before," said Clarke's manager, Andrew "Chubby" Chandler, "but it usually only happens once every three years." But when it does, watch out. After a level-par outward half, Clarke birdied the 12th from eight feet and otherwise parred on relentlessly.

"Obviously, if someone had given me a 69 before I was going out to play, I would have bitten their hand off," Clarke said. "Saying that, we did get very fortunate with the draw. To win any tournament, the draw can make a difference, but in The Open Championship it makes a huge difference. We got very lucky. We started in terrible conditions and then it sort of cleared up after four or five holes, so we got lucky with the weather again."

Excerpts FROM THE Press

"The Weather Channel is missing an opportunity…. Think of what fun it could have had with maps and charts and tornado chasers, zipping up and down the fairways of Royal St George's fabled golf course and reporting back."

—**Bill Dwyre**, *Los Angeles Times*

"The most impressive thing came in the eye of a monsoon when a 61-year-old man gave everyone another lesson in links golf. When it comes to outwitting the field, the course, and the surrounding storm, it's elementary for Tom Watson."

—**Scott Michaux**, *Augusta Chronicle*

"By the end of his round, Bo Van Pelt looked like he had spent his Saturday stuck inside a dishwasher during the rinse cycle. 'Brutal,' he said."

—**Gene Wojciechowski, ESPN.com**

"Sergio Garcia says he is drawing on the spirit of Seve Ballesteros at Royal St George's. He says his mind 'wanders here and there on Seve' as he sees the billboards featuring the Spanish legend. It's helping — the 31-year-old is still in the hunt as he seeks a maiden Major."

—**Neil Squires**, *Sunday Express*

"Englishman Paul Casey disappeared for a 'nice cup of tea' after finishing eight over in the third round at Royal St George's. It left him 11 over for the tournament and, after his tea, he could only offer sympathy for the fans that followed him around in unrelenting rain."

—**Steve Millar**, *Daily Star Sunday*

Third Round Leaders

HOLE	1	2	3	4	5	6	7	8	9	10	11	12	13	14	15	16	17	18	
PAR	4	4	3	4	4	3	5	4	4	4	3	4	4	5	4	3	4	4	TOTAL
Darren Clarke	(3)	4	3	4	[5]	3	(4)	[5]	4	4	3	(3)	4	5	4	3	4	4	69-205
Dustin Johnson	4	4	3	[5]	(3)	3	(4)	4	[5]	(3)	3	(3)	[5]	(4)	(3)	3	[5]	4	68-206
Rickie Fowler	4	[5]	3	4	(3)	3	5	4	4	4	[4]	4	(3)	5	(3)	(2)	4	4	68-208
Thomas Bjorn	4	(3)	3	[5]	4	[4]	(4)	4	4	4	3	4	4	5	4	3	[5]	4	71-208
Miguel Angel Jimenez	4	4	3	[5]	4	[4]	5	4	4	4	3	4	4	5	4	3	4	4	72-209
Lucas Glover	[5]	4	3	4	4	3	5	4	4	4	3	[5]	4	5	4	3	[5]	4	73-209
Anthony Kim	[5]	4	3	[5]	[5]	3	5	[5]	(3)	4	3	(3)	4	(4)	(3)	3	4	4	70-210
Phil Mickelson	4	4	[4]	[5]	4	[4]	(4)	4	4	[5]	(2)	4	(4)	4	3	4	4	71-210
Anders Hansen	4	4	3	[5]	4	[4]	(4)	[5]	(2)	4	3	4	4	5	4	3	4	[6]	72-210
George Coetzee	4	4	3	[5]	4	[4]	(4)	4	(3)	4	[4]	4	4	(4)	[6]	3	4	4	72-210
Davis Love III	[5]	4	[4]	4	4	3	(4)	4	4	4	(2)	4	[5]	5	4	3	[5]	4	72-210
Martin Kaymer	4	4	[4]	4	4	[4]	[6]	4	4	4	[4]	4	(3)	(4)	[5]	3	4	4	73-210

Thomas Bjorn said of his 71: 'It was tough out there today, so you've got to be happy with that.'

Lucas Glover returned a 73 with three bogeys, falling to a tie for fifth place.

Clarke and Glover teed-off at 3.05 and the weather did indeed start to clear up, as forecast, around 4pm. The leaders may have got lucky, but they earned it by playing the best over the first two days. "The guys who played this morning must feel hard done by," said Bjorn. "They would have gotten up this morning thinking they hardly had a chance of making a move. Then the rain went away for us after five or six holes. I wouldn't say it ever became easy, but it was more pleasant out there."

Johnson teed-off 50 minutes before Clarke and Glover and so had easier conditions on the inward nine, but Fowler teed-off at 12.35 alongside Rory McIlroy and they only had a handful of holes at the end when conditions eased. If Fowler's was the round of the day, the best battling effort came from an old stager. Tom Watson teed-off at 10.30 in the

George Coetzee said: 'I'm here to compare myself to the best.'

"

"It was tough.... There was a moment when Bubba (Watson) and I looked at each other and started laughing."

—Jason Day

"It was a fun day. It was certainly challenging with the rain. We got lucky. I think the guys who played late got really lucky, myself included."

—Phil Mickelson

"It's unfortunate. You would like to see it even out as far as conditions go with the whole field, but it's just the luck of the draw."

—Zach Johnson

"This week has been full of tough conditions, but today, I've only seen this one time in my life, a tougher day, and that was at Muirfield in 2002."

—Stewart Cink

"I've found my game, it's just I haven't brought it to tournaments. I'm excited that this is the tournament I brought it to."

—Anthony Kim

"It was a bad day, so hopefully I can learn from my mistakes out there."

—Tom Lewis

"

Martin Kaymer posted a 73 after being four over through 11 holes.

10th group of the day, and the 72 he returned was the lowest to be returned so far and was around five strokes below the early morning average. His four-over 214 was the clubhouse lead for much of the afternoon.

It was vintage Watson, and those like Fowler who watched some of the television coverage before venturing outside needed to look no further for their inspiration. "He looked like he was having fun, smiling and embracing the conditions," Fowler said. Watson said it was the sort of conditions that could "tear you up and spit you out."

Zach Johnson, returning a 71, made 4 from the rough on the first and overcame a 6 on the fourth.

While Fowler's generation had not experienced the like, Watson did not think the conditions were as bad as at Muirfield in 2002 or, indeed, 1980.

"When conditions are bothersome you just try to keep the grips dry, keep your wits about you, and go about your business to try and make par. Par is a great score out there," he said. There were quite a few Watson pars. He holed good putts at the first and the fourth, where he had hit two drivers and was still short, and after a birdie at the par-5 seventh he was still one under par after 10 holes. There were four bogeys in the last eight holes, as well as a 2 at the 16th, but it did not detract from one of the great bad weather rounds in The Open.

Matthew Millar, from Australia, was the first man out as a single and returned an 80. Paul Lawrie, the 1999 Champion from Carnoustie, had an 81, as did American Spencer Levin. South Korea's Jung-Gon Hwang had an 83. Lawrie achieved one of the day's

Anthony Kim had a 70 with 32 on the inward nine.

Round of the **Day**

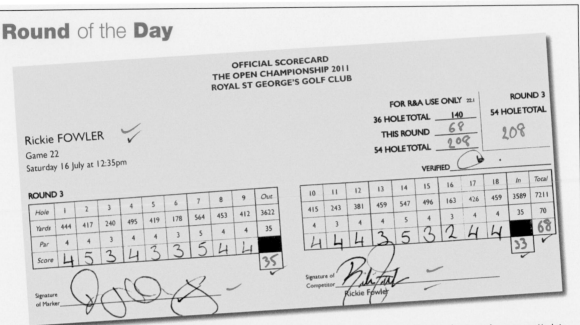

Rickie FOWLER
Game 22
Saturday 16 July at 12:35pm

FOR R&A USE ONLY 22.1

36 HOLE TOTAL _140_
THIS ROUND _68_
54 HOLE TOTAL _208_

ROUND 3
54 HOLE TOTAL _208_

VERIFIED _____

ROUND 3

Hole	1	2	3	4	5	6	7	8	9	Out	10	11	12	13	14	15	16	17	18	In	Total
Yards	444	417	240	495	419	178	564	453	412	3622	415	243	381	459	547	496	163	426	459	3589	7211
Par	4	4	3	4	4	3	5	4	4	35	4	4	4	4	5	4	3	4	4	35	70
Score	4	5	3	4	3	3	5	4	4	35	4	4	4	3	5	3	2	4	4	33	68

Signature of Marker _____

Signature of Competitor _____
Rickie Fowler

It was just his second Open, but Rickie Fowler adjusted like a veteran to the wind and rain of the third day. He was off at 12.35pm, two and a half hours ahead of the final game, and in the worst of the weather. The harsh conditions persisted in full force through Fowler's first nine holes then gradually subsided.

Fowler's 68, along with that of Dustin Johnson, who went off at 2.15pm, were the lowest scores of the day.

After a par on the first hole, Fowler was in two bunkers and took bogey at the second. He scored a birdie on the fifth with a wedge shot to 15 feet and made the turn in level-par 35. He dropped a shot on the 11th hole, but then finished with three birdies — with a 9-iron to 15 feet at the 13th, a 6-iron to 12 feet at the 15th, and another 6-iron to 20 feet at the 16th.

"I was very much in control of my game,

and it was nice to make some putts late in the round there," Fowler said. "You have to embrace where you are and what's in front of you. My caddie and I were trying to keep moving forward and to stay positive. We knew it was going to be tough to make any birdies out there today. But when you make the best of it and go at it with the right attitude, 68 is possible. But I had to play pretty well to do that."

Low Scores

Low First Nine
Gary Woodland — 33

Low Second Nine
Anthony Kim — 32

Low Round
Dustin Johnson — 68
Rickie Fowler — 68

two eagles, at the seventh, but also had a 7 at the fourth after finding the Himalaya bunker. Levin had an 8. Gary Woodland, one of the game's biggest hitters, made the first par of the round on the fourth at the sixth attempt. Although the tee was moved up 25 yards, most players could only hit their drives around 200 yards and ended up playing it as a par 5. Indeed, at the end of the day it averaged 4.93 and there were no birdies recorded at all, although the short third, the eighth, and the 18th were also devoid of feathery delight.

Another frightening hole was the 14th, with the wind blowing left-to-right and bringing the out of bounds into play on the right. McIlroy was one of those to hit onto the Prince's course. "You've got half of Kent on your left and I went right, it was disappointing," McIlroy said. France's Gregory Havret had a 10, and the hole averaged 5.23 for the day rather than under par as usual.

Rickie Fowler showed a 68 was 'possible. But I had to play pretty well to do that.'

Edoardo Molinari said he hit a drive and a 2-iron short of the green at the 10th, having been 30 yards short of the green with his drive on Thursday. The short 16th, playing 157 yards, was routinely played with a 4-iron. "It was like going 18 holes with the heavyweight champion of the world," said Trevor Immelman, who was the second player to return a 72.

Bubba Watson and Jason Day could not believe how many people were out watching. "We were talking to the fans and asking, 'Why are y'all out here? Why aren't you watching on TV?' They love the sport that much they're out here cheering us on," said Bubba. Lawrie said: "There were 40 or 50 people walking with us, and I said to them, 'You're just mental.' I just don't understand that at all. I'm getting paid. I've got to be here." What players thought of getting to the 14th tee and seeing people playing at Prince's, having paid for the privilege, is unprintable.

Excerpts FROM THE Press

"Rickie Fowler stuck out amid the greyness as hard, sideways rain led to an early exit for some steely British golf fans. The ones who stayed surely appreciated Fowler more for the way he fought through the conditions to post a dazzling 68 than his cream-colored rainsuit with pink polka dots."
—Tim Dahlberg, *The Associated Press*

"Darren Clarke's performance was characterised by the things he has always done so well. Though he drove the ball beautifully, the priceless key was superb iron play. With the familiar, abbreviated followthrough, he worked the ball with obvious relish over tricky, windswept terrain for a round which contained only two bogeys."
—Dermot Gilleece, *Sunday Independent*

"(Veteran caddie) Joe LaCava downplays what benefit he brings to Dustin Johnson as he heads into the final round at The Open Championship in the final group with Darren Clarke. But his steadying presence and experience certainly can be of value."
—Bob Harig, ESPN.com

"Rickie Fowler got his first exposure to links golf at the 2007 Walker Cup, as the youngest member of a United States team travelling to Royal County Down in Ireland. The kid's a fast learner."
—Jeff Shain, *Orlando Sentinel*

Tom Lehman, the 1996 Champion, had a 73 that featured a finish of bogey, birdie, bogey.

Andres Hansen posted a 72 with 6 on the last hole.

For the third day running, Fowler and McIlroy were playing together. By now it was becoming apparent that the young American has a flair for links golf and is completely comfortable playing in the wind. McIlroy, who may have played a lot at Royal County Down but whose home course of Holywood is an inland parkland track, is not. He bogeyed the first and the third holes and had a double-bogey at the 14th after hitting his second shot out of bounds. There was only a single birdie in his 74.

Fowler, on the other hand, kept to the task in hand like a veteran and was rewarded with three birdies in four holes from the 13th. The one hole he did not birdie was the par-5 14th. He holed from 15 feet at the 13th, 12 feet at the 15th, and from 20 feet at the 16th after hitting a 6-iron in. It added up to an inward 33. "It was awesome out there," said the 22-year-old. "I felt very in control of my game and it was nice to make some putts late in the round. Given the situation and the tournament,

Major Questions
Johnson Believes He Has Answers

Good as it was, Dustin Johnson's 68 on Saturday raised more questions than it answered. His 54-hole total of 206, four under par, was one stroke behind Darren Clarke, the leader, and brought echoes of recent previous Major Championships. It was the third time in the past six Major Championships that Johnson had put himself into contention.

Suddenly came the questions about the 2010 US Open when he had led by three strokes after three rounds and disappeared from contention with an 82 in the fourth round; the questions about last year's PGA Championship where he had led by one stroke on the 18th tee only to be penalised two strokes on that hole for grounding his club in a sandy area.

"What do you take from your past experiences in the Majors?" Johnson was asked at Sandwich. "Does it make a difference to be the one chasing?" "Does it help that you're not going into this one with the outright lead bearing in mind the experiences you've had in the past?"

Johnson dealt with them all much as he had dealt with the foul weather that marked the third day and much as he had dealt with the swollen glands a local doctor had diagnosed on the eve of the Championship. He got on with things, not dwelling on any dark thoughts of the past, and moving steadily up the field with such success that after going four over par for his first 10 holes on Thursday he had climbed back and now only Clarke was ahead of him.

"It doesn't matter whether you're chasing or got the lead," Johnson said. "I would rather have the lead because it is one shot less I have to make up, but going out tomorrow I am still going to have to play aggressive when I can and play smart when I have to. I've been in this situation a few times and I think the more you can put yourself in a situation the more comfortable you get. I am going to be pretty comfortable out there, because I know what to expect.

"It is still the final group of a Major Championship, so it is not going to feel any different. At the US Open I struggled. It was the first time I had gone into a Major in the last group. I had a really good warm-up, so I wasn't expecting to go out and play bad. In the PGA, other than the last hole I played really good golf."

Johnson had plenty of support from his countrymen and this went against current form in that Americans had not won a Major Championship since Phil Mickelson did so at Augusta in 2010. Royal St George's might be a course named after England's patron saint in Kent, a county known as the Garden of England overlooking the English Channel, but it was Americans not Englishmen who were packing the leaderboard. There were two Americans in the top three, six in the top seven, and 14 in the top 25.

"Dustin really doesn't think about a whole lot," said Rickie Fowler, who was one stroke behind Johnson, sharing third place with Thomas Bjorn. "He's someone that gets over things pretty quickly. He's a great player. I love the way he plays the game. I wouldn't worry about Dustin. He'll be fine."

—**John Hopkins**

where I'm at in my career, that's probably the worst conditions I've played in and the best I've played in those conditions."

Yet to win as a professional, Fowler had nonetheless made the US Ryder Cup team as a rookie in 2010. The climax to his match in the singles against Edoardo Molinari when he birdied the last four holes to get a half, and keep the overall contest alive right to the last match on the course, showed he is made of the right stuff. "That's probably something I can draw on for the rest of my life," he said.

Fowler's four birdies were matched by Anthony Kim, and the only person to have more was their compatriot Johnson with six. On the

Third Round Scores	
Players Under Par	3
Players At Par	1
Players Over Par	67

Excerpts FROM THE Press

"Darren Clarke escaped the worst of the raging weather in The Open, leaving him far less traffic on his unlikely road to a Claret Jug."

—**Doug Ferguson,** *The Associated Press*

"This is a week when every fibre of a golfer's being is tested and every weakness exposed, be it technical or mental. If there's a flaw in your driving or your iron play or your chipping or your putting, then you will be found out in places like this."

—**Tom English,** *Scotland on Sunday*

"The expensively equipped European Tour physiotherapy truck looking after players at The Open offers massages for aching backs but could do nothing to help the bruised egos that have trudged off Royal St George's in the past three days."

—**Graham Otway,**
The Independent on Sunday

"Yes, they are over here, over excited, and overdue. The leaderboard resembled the Kent coast in wartime. Blighty, awash with Yanks talking big and eyeing the prettiest prize in golf."

—**Kevin Garside,**
The Sunday Telegraph

"After a round of casual brilliance, and in the evening of his career, Darren Clarke has a wonderful opportunity to crown his golfing life with victory in The Open Championship."

—**Nick Pitt,** *The Sunday Times*

Simon Dyson posted a second 72.

Raphael Jacquelin returned a 71.

Webb Simpson's 72 included 5 on the first and 7 on the 14th.

inward nine he picked up shots at the 10th, where he holed from 10 feet, the 12th, thanks to a 25-footer finding the cup, the 14th, after finding the front edge in two, and the 15th, where he hit a 9-iron to a foot. Only a bogey at the 17th, where his approach found the bunker on the right, stopped him sharing the 54-hole lead with Clarke.

Like Fowler, Johnson described how much he enjoyed the challenge of links golf. Unlike Fowler, Johnson had won on the PGA Tour. In fact he had won four times, but twice he had led going into the last round of a Major in 2010 and neither time had turned out well. At the US Open he collapsed to an 82, while at the US PGA Championship

Round Three Hole Summary

HOLE	PAR	YARDS	EAGLES	BIRDIES	PARS	BOGEYS	D.BOGEYS	HIGHER	RANK	AVERAGE
1	4	444	0	1	52	18	0	0	10	4.24
2	4	417	0	4	49	18	0	0	12	4.20
3	3	240	0	0	40	31	0	0	4	3.44
4	4	495	0	0	18	43	8	2	1	4.93
5	4	419	0	9	50	12	0	0	17	4.04
6	3	178	0	3	40	27	1	0	6	3.37
7	5	564	1	35	33	2	0	0	18	4.51
8	4	453	0	0	35	31	5	0	2	4.58
9	4	412	1	8	43	17	2	0	13	4.15
OUT	**35**	**3,622**	**2**	**60**	**360**	**199**	**16**	**2**		**37.45**
10	4	415	0	4	44	22	1	0	8	4.28
11	3	243	0	5	43	23	0	0	9	3.25
12	4	381	0	8	48	15	0	0	15	4.10
13	4	459	0	11	43	16	1	0	15	4.10
14	5	547	0	13	41	10	4	3	11	5.23
15	4	496	0	5	39	23	4	0	5	4.37
16	3	163	0	5	52	14	0	0	14	3.13
17	4	426	0	2	47	21	1	0	7	4.30
18	4	459	0	0	40	27	4	0	3	4.49
IN	**35**	**3,589**	**0**	**53**	**397**	**171**	**15**	**3**		**37.24**
TOTAL	**70**	**7,211**	**2**	**113**	**757**	**370**	**31**	**5**		**74.69**

he was still leading playing the last but grounded his club in an area he did not realise was designated a bunker. The playoff between Martin Kaymer and Bubba Watson went on without him.

Now he would be playing in the final pairing of a Major for the third time in just over a year. "I think the more you can put yourself in this situation, the more comfortable you get," said the 27-year-old. "I know how to approach it."

As one of the longest hitters of the younger generation, Johnson's display of links know-how was intriguing. But Phil Mickelson did not think it was surprising. "There are a lot of holes you can play along the ground here, but most of the holes on the front you have to carry," Mickelson said. "On two you have to hit over the bunkers, same on four, at five you are trying to drive over the hill, and over the mounds on seven. The longer and higher you hit it, the better off you are.

With a 72, Davis Love III was on level-par 210.

Steve Stricker had an inward 35 for his 72.

Louis Oosthuizen soared to a 74, four over.

It's a Fact

With three rounds under 70 in the 2011 Open, Darren Clarke has 25 rounds under 70 in his 20-year Open career. He shares sixth place in that category with Nick Price and Mark Calcavecchia. These are the top five: Sir Nick Faldo (37 rounds under 70), Ernie Els (36), Jack Nicklaus (33), Tom Watson (29), and Greg Norman (26).

"So his length is allowing him to take advantage of the holes that are reachable with the wind and he's making birdies. I played a practice round with him and on 17 he drove the green. So you give him a little bit of helping wind and he can hit it over 400 yards."

Mickelson himself had a 71 to be level par. Playing alongside the young amateur Tom Lewis, who was disappointed with a 76 to be five over par, Mickelson had four bogeys in his first 10 holes but played the last eight in two under. "It was certainly challenging with the rain, but we got lucky and it went away around the turn," he said. "We went from really fighting to make pars on every hole to thinking birdies on some."

In a tie for seventh place, Lefty was still lurking with intent. "There is nothing more exciting on a Sunday than having a chance in a Major," Mickelson said. "I know I'm not leading, but I'm also right there. If I can play a good solid round of a couple under par, I don't know how many, maybe six, maybe two, depends on the weather, I'm going to have a good chance tomorrow. To me that is so much

Adam Scott finished with a 73, having birdies on the 10th and 14th holes.

fun and I'm excited. I feel like it is my first time over here."

Other lurkers on level par included US PGA Champion Kaymer, Davis Love III, who was fourth in 2003, Kim, Anders Hansen, who eagled the ninth by holing a sand wedge but had a double-bogey at the last, and South Africa's George Coetzee. Who would come out of the pack and attack the lead the following day?

But at day's end the attention was on Clarke. He had been the halfway leader at Royal Troon in 1997, but both he and Jesper Parnevik were overtaken by Justin Leonard and they finished as the joint runners-up, three behind. Then in 2001 Clarke was third to David Duval after contending down the stretch. In 19 previous attempts at The Open, those were his closest calls. It took Padraig Harrington 11 attempts to win the Claret Jug and Sir Nick Faldo 12. Nick Price won on his 16th attempt in 1994, but no one had tried more often and won his first Open.

"Obviously, I'm very excited," Clarke said. "The Open is the biggest and best tournament in the world. As you know, I've failed 19 times to lift the Claret Jug and tomorrow I have another opportunity. But at the moment it's just an opportunity because the weather is going to be very windy again tomorrow and there's a long way to go still

In the Words of the Competitors...

"

"I made it worse than it was. I three-putted twice in the first four holes, so I made the worst of a bad situation. It's a shame but I rallied hard. I played really nicely on the back nine."

—Adam Scott

"About three or four people in the field can hit the ball 250 yards in a howling gale. Apart from that, it was brutal."

—Paul Lawrie

"Conditions were very difficult. The first few holes were probably the toughest we had for the 18 holes, and our first four or five holes were pretty tough."

—Steve Stricker

"With the way I started, I'm very pleased. I was four over through 10 holes, not hitting it well."

—Louis Oosthuizen

"Plus one today feels under par, and I'm very happy about that."

—Raphael Jacquelin

"It seems in this tournament, more than anything else, you need to get a good draw, and it just hasn't worked out for me this week."

—Rory McIlroy

With a 76, Jason Day tumbled to a tie for 41st.

Charl Schwartzel recorded a 75 with two 6s.

Chad Campbell had an inward 38 for a 74.

in this Championship. But I'm very pleased to be leading going into the last round."

After the Ryder Cup at The K Club in 2006, just weeks after the death of his wife Heather, Clarke always said that nothing could feel worse on the golf course. Here was his first chance to prove the theory. It had been a long wait. "Did I ever doubt I would get myself back in this position? No. Did I know it was going to happen? No. Did I hope it was going to happen? Yes. But did I ever doubt it? No."

As for the waiting until his final round tee-time, Clarke said: "I can while away the time very easily. That doesn't bother me in the slightest. Tonight I'll go to Chubby's, where there are some fantastic chefs, and stuff my face and go to bed at about 10 o'clock and try not to drink too much. Tomorrow morning, I'll probably get up and stuff my face again. I'll just relax and watch a little bit of the golf or whatever, but I'll be fine."

The Rory and Rickie Show

By Art Spander

Rory McIlroy showed up at Royal St George's with a US Open Championship, claimed in record fashion three weeks earlier, the attention of all of Europe, and even more stories in the dailies than William and Kate, whose tour of North America was headline stuff.

Reportedly two bets of £20,000 had been made on McIlroy, who when asked if the wagers were the acts of shrewd punters or desperate men replied: "I'll go for the first option."

The first two days of The Open, McIlroy was grouped with Ernie Els, a three-time Major Championship winner and surely one of the game's greats if at age 41 a bit on the downside, and Rickie Fowler, who at 22, the same age as McIlroy, kept being mentioned in terms of potential.

Four years earlier, in the Walker Cup at Royal County Down in Northern Ireland, one of McIlroy's home courses, Fowler and Billy Horschel had teamed to defeat McIlroy and Jonny Caldwell, 2 and 1 in foursomes. A friendship and a rivalry began.

"It's fun playing with someone you enjoy being around," said Fowler, "but at the same time we're trying to beat each other." Which, through two rounds of the 2011 Open, neither was able to accomplish, McIlroy, with all the pressure, returning 71-69–140, level par, and Fowler, with all the hopes, having 70-70–140.

And so for a third day, through the result of their own play, not the creation of the draw, they would be together, four shots behind co-leaders Darren Clarke and Lucas Glover in what was being labelled the championship within the Championship.

The rains and wind had been present through the morning. And logic decreed McIlroy, who grew up near Belfast in this sort of weather, would be better prepared for the conditions than Fowler, who until he went to university at Oklahoma State spent his life hitting golf balls and racing dirt bikes in the California sunshine near Los Angeles.

On the contrary. Fowler handled the

downpour and gusts as beautifully as the weather for a while was awful. Fowler had watched Tom Watson on television battle gleefully through the storm before it was his time to tee-off. "He just saw how (Watson) looked like he was having fun, smiling and embracing the conditions," Joe Skovron, Fowler's caddie, told David Walsh of *The Sunday Times*. "You know the best way to deal with them is to go out and make a good time of it."

Fowler, in his white weather proofs with polka-dots, his white flat-brim hat with the oversized Puma logo in blue on the side, occasionally keeping his hands warm and dry with huge mittens which looked like the sort a baker utilizes to pull bread out of the ovens, made a wonderful time of it. He was even par with a birdie and bogey on the front, then two under on the back for a 68 which tied fellow American Dustin Johnson for low round of the day.

McIlroy, the focus of the fans who were waiting for Clarke an hour and a half later, missed the first two fairways. Although he hung in through 13 holes, he and the gallery sensed he would come in second in this two-man competition. Later, McIlroy would bemoan his fate, saying, "I am not a fan of

golf tournaments where the outcome is predicted so much by the weather, it is not my sort of golf."

It is, however, at times very much a part of Open Championship golf. A year earlier at St Andrews, McIlroy opened with a 63, blew to 80 when the wind blew so hard Friday play had to be suspended, then rallied in more benign conditions to tie for third.

McIlroy came to grief on the 14th hole, a 547-yard par 5 named Suez Canal because of a narrow stream crossing the fairway and out of bounds to the right over a low fence which divides Royal St George's and Prince's Golf Club. Rory hit a bad shot but later followed it with a great quote.

Whack. There went the ball. There went any chances. "I mean, you've done so well for 13 holes to keep yourself in it," McIlroy sighed, "and then to hit... you've got half of Kent on your left, and you hit it right."

McIlroy would finish at 74, six behind Fowler, who gained McIlroy's admiration for doing what Rory was unable to do. "Rickie played really well," said McIlroy, ever the sportsman. "He's such a natural player, and he's got a lot of feel, so he controls the ball very well. He's got a great short game. He gets it up and down when he needs to, holes good putts on the right holes."

Fowler definitely did that in the 2010 Ryder Cup at Celtic Manor. Four down with four to play against Edoardo Molinari, Fowler birdied 15, 16, 17, and 18 for a half. He said he will draw from that match "the rest of his life." As he will from beating McIlroy and the course the third day of The Open.

"Where I am in my career," Fowler said after Saturday at Royal St George's, "it was probably the worst conditions I've played in and the best I've played in those conditions."

On that day, better than his friend Rory McIlroy and as well as anyone in the tournament.

Fourth Round

Clarke Claims His Claret Jug

By Andy Farrell

On his 20th attempt Darren Clarke, known as the golfer's golfer, becomes a most popular Champion Golfer of the Year.

In his own words, "a bit of a normal bloke" won the 2011 Open Championship. But there was nothing normal about the golf Darren Clarke played at Royal St George's this week. It was a demonstration of the art of links golf of the very highest order, performed on a course and in weather conditions that most of his competitors felt made for a "brutal" combination. Such was his superiority that Clarke had four putts for the title on the 72nd green. Such was the intensity with which the gallery was willing him to victory that when the first of them did not find the hole, a nervous sigh seeped from the grandstands.

Clarke looked up, muttered something along the lines that "it doesn't matter," and tapped in from a mere three inches. Instantly, the roars that had followed Clarke around Sandwich for four days erupted again. Arms aloft, he accepted the acclaim with a smile that could not be broader had he already been handed the Claret Jug or, indeed, a pint of Guinness. Clarke was long acknowledged as the golfer's golfer. Now, finally, he was announced as the Champion Golfer of the Year. "It's been a dream since I was a kid to win The Open," he said. "It feels incredible right now."

Clarke had said he would be fine whiling away the hours before the last tee-time of the final round, and he was aided by some pertinent advice via text message from his old friend Tiger Woods. He was certainly fine once he had holed from 12 feet for a par at the first hole. Throughout the afternoon, the wind gusted, pulses of torrential rain kept sweeping across the links, and challengers threatened his lead, but Clarke repulsed them all.

Phil Mickelson produced the most brilliant charge to tie briefly for the lead and was six under par for his first 10 holes before missing a short putt at the 11th. Dustin Johnson took up the assault but went out of bounds at the 14th. The big man from Portrush was at his sturdiest best. To eagle the seventh, as Mickelson had done moments before, to

---

Arms aloft, Darren Clarke received his acclaim with a smile.

Phil Mickelson said of his putt at the seventh: 'I'm not planning on making a 50-footer for eagle, it just happens.'

Low Scores	
Low First Nine	
Phil Mickelson	30
Low Second Nine	
Chad Campbell	34
Steve Stricker	34
Martin Kaymer	34
Low Round	
Phil Mickelson	68
Sergio Garcia	68

re-establish a two-stroke lead was the highlight of the round, but the nine pars in a row that followed was the resolution that ultimately broke his rivals.

A pair of bogeys at the last two holes mattered only to reduce his winning margin over Mickelson and Johnson to three strokes and stopped Clarke from becoming only the fourth Champion to record all four rounds in the 60s. After scores of 68, 68, and 69, his final round of 70 gave him a winning total of 275, five under par. Mickelson, after a 68 that matched Sergio Garcia for the lowest score of the day, and Johnson, following a 72, finished at two under. Thomas Bjorn was the only other player to finish under par for the week after closing with a 71.

At the age of 42, Clarke was the oldest Champion since the 44-year-old Roberto de Vicenzo in 1967. He was only the second winner from Northern Ireland, 64 years after Fred Daly won in 1947 at Hoylake. It had been all of a month since the country's last Major triumph by Rory McIlroy at the US Open and its third in six Majors since Graeme McDowell won at Pebble Beach in 2010. While celebrating

Fourth Round Leaders

HOLE	1	2	3	4	5	6	7	8	9	10	11	12	13	14	15	16	17	18	
PAR	4	4	3	4	4	3	5	4	4	4	3	4	4	5	4	3	4	4	TOTAL
Darren Clarke	4	(3)	3	[5]	4	3	(3)	4	4	4	3	4	4	5	4	3	[5]	[5]	70-275
Phil Mickelson	4	(3)	3	(3)	4	(2)	(3)	4	4	(3)	[4]	4	[5]	5	[5]	[4]	4	4	68-278
Dustin Johnson	4	4	[4]	4	4	[4]	(4)	4	4	(3)	3	(3)	4	[7]	4	3	4	[5]	72-278
Thomas Bjorn	4	4	3	[5]	4	(2)	5	(3)	4	4	3	4	4	5	[5]	3	[5]	4	71-279
Chad Campbell	[5]	(3)	(2)	4	4	3	(4)	[5]	[5]	4	3	(3)	4	5	4	[4]	4	(3)	69-280
Anthony Kim	4	(3)	3	[5]	4	3	(4)	4	4	4	3	(3)	4	5	[5]	3	4	[5]	70-280
Rickie Fowler	4	4	3	4	4	3	5	4	4	4	3	4	4	[6]	4	[4]	4	4	72-280
Raphael Jacquelin	(3)	4	3	4	4	3	5	4	(3)	4	[4]	4	4	(4)	[5]	(2)	[5]	4	69-281
Sergio Garcia	4	(3)	3	(3)	(3)	3	(4)	[6]	4	4	3	4	[5]	5	4	(2)	[5]	(3)	68-282
Simon Dyson	4	4	[4]	4	4	[4]	(3)	(3)	[5]	[5]	3	4	4	(4)	4	3	4	4	70-282
Davis Love III	[5]	(3)	[4]	4	4	3	(4)	[5]	4	4	3	4	4	5	[5]	3	4	4	72-282

Following Mickelson's eagle, Clarke struck an 8-iron at the seventh from 198 yards and holed a 16-foot eagle putt.

Dustin Johnson, chipping here at the third, carried his challenge to the 14th hole, where he hit out of bounds.

Chad Campbell posted a 69 to tie for fifth place.

those achievements, there had been those who had told the old man to get his finger out: from mentor to Champion.

"We're blessed to have two fantastic players in Rory and G-Mac, and I'm just the old guy coming along behind them," Clarke said. "We're lucky. We have fantastic courses and fantastic facilities, but to have three Major Champions from such a small place in a short period of time is incredible. It's brilliant for home. They'll all be very pleased. We are a very close-knit community and everyone is pleased when our sporting guys do well."

Yet however much Clarke's victory was celebrated back at home, the affection with which the galleries in Kent cheered him on was genuinely heart-felt. He was the first home winner of The Open since Paul Lawrie in 1999, and the scenes must have

Showing thanks to the crowd, Thomas Bjorn was fourth on 279.

been reminiscent of Henry Cotton winning at Sandwich in 1934 and Sandy Lyle in 1985. Almost 40,000 spectators lined the fairways on Sunday, making 179,700 for the week despite uninviting weather at the weekend, and to a man, woman, and child Clarke was the hero. "They were sensational for me all week," he acknowledged. "The support they have given me through the bad weather as well as the good was just brilliant. They were all roaring and shouting. They have been very kind to me."

Walking off the 18th green, there were a series of emotional embraces. First was John Mulrooney, his Irish caddie who helped him win in Mallorca two months earlier but had arrived at Sandwich having experienced Clarke at his petulant worst the previous Sunday in the final round of the Barclays Scottish Open. Then there were his parents, Godfrey, a greenkeeper at Dungannon when Darren was first learning the game, and Hattie, who described her son's decision to move back to Portrush with his sons Tyrone and Conor a year earlier the best of his life. His fiancée Alison was next, and then came a mighty bear-hug for his manager and close friend Andrew "Chubby" Chandler.

Excerpts FROM THE Press

"Darren Clarke, Open Champion. Easy to say, hard to believe. But that was the story told as the big man from Dungannon walked strong and proud through the squalls, all the way up the final hole theatre at Royal St George's to claim the greatest prize in golf."

—**Lawrence Donegan,** *The Guardian*

"Don't they erect statues for performances as epic as this?"

—**Derek Lawrenson,** *Daily Mail*

"Well, that was quite an Open wasn't it? While there were no doubt some scandal-starved, tabloid-minded point-missers who walked away calling their week in Kent 'flat' or 'boring' because no insults were flying … this was a Championship for the connoisseurs of links golf, those with a true appreciation for the finest and most interesting form of the greatest game. We had it all, really."

—**John Huggan,** *Scotland on Sunday*

"In the United States, where Major Championships were once a birthright, what memories remain? Phil Mickelson's thrilling ride to a tie for the lead with an eagle at the seventh? That was marred by … well, pick one from a bevy of miscues."

—**Barry Svrluga,** *The Washington Post*

In his Sunday orange (for Oklahoma State University), Rickie Fowler returned a 72 to tie for fifth on 280, level par.

Anthony Kim bogeyed two of the last four for 280.

Waiting his turn was Mickelson, who has become a close friend since his wife and mother were diagnosed with breast cancer. Clarke had been the first person on the phone and they had talked many times. "I couldn't be happier for him," said the American. "There are a lot of players who are extremely happy for him. He is very well liked."

At the presentation ceremony, where he thanked The R&A and the Royal St George's greenkeeping staff for producing a perfectly conditioned course, and again in the press conference afterwards, Clarke made reference to his late wife Heather, who died from breast cancer in 2006. "To sit here and talk in front of you guys with this trophy, being the Open Champion, just means the world to me," Clarke said in the Media Centre.

"In terms of what's going through my heart, there's obviously somebody who is watching down from up above there, and I know she would be very proud of me. She'd probably be saying, 'I told you so.' But I think she'd be more proud of my

Round Four Hole Summary

HOLE	PAR	YARDS	EAGLES	BIRDIES	PARS	BOGEYS	D.BOGEYS	HIGHER	RANK	AVERAGE
1	4	444	0	3	55	13	0	0	14	4.14
2	4	417	0	20	47	4	0	0	17	3.77
3	3	240	0	3	42	24	2	0	5	3.35
4	4	495	0	2	34	30	4	1	1	4.55
5	4	419	0	10	52	8	1	0	16	4.00
6	3	178	0	7	45	17	2	0	12	3.20
7	5	564	8	33	24	6	0	0	18	4.39
8	4	453	0	8	38	18	6	1	5	4.35
9	4	412	0	6	44	18	2	1	8	4.27
OUT	**35**	**3,622**	**8**	**92**	**381**	**138**	**17**	**3**		**36.03**
10	4	415	0	5	39	20	7	0	3	4.41
11	3	243	0	7	45	18	1	0	13	3.18
12	4	381	0	8	51	12	0	0	15	4.06
13	4	459	0	5	47	18	1	0	11	4.21
14	5	547	0	10	43	13	2	3	8	5.27
15	4	496	0	1	45	22	2	1	4	4.39
16	3	163	0	9	38	22	2	0	10	3.24
17	4	426	0	1	38	27	5	0	2	4.51
18	4	459	0	5	40	25	1	0	7	4.31
IN	**35**	**3,589**	**0**	**51**	**386**	**177**	**21**	**4**		**37.58**
TOTAL	**70**	**7,211**	**8**	**143**	**767**	**315**	**38**	**7**		**73.61**

two boys and them at home watching more than anything else. It's been a long journey to get here. I'm 42 and I'm not getting any younger.

"But I got here in the end. It may be the only Major that I win, it may not be. But at least I went out there and did my best and my best was good enough to win. If I had come off and hadn't won, I could still say I did my best. I ask my two boys to do their best and that's what they do. I can't ask them for any more, so I think their dad should try and do the same."

Amid such emotional sentiments, Clarke said it was only when he was walking onto the green at the last that he let his thoughts turn away from the job in hand. "At that stage I had four putts for it and I figured I could manage that. I certainly had a few thoughts going through my head, thinking of the past. If I didn't feel a little bit emotional it wouldn't be right. I just managed to cling on."

Raphael Jacquelin's 69 placed him eighth on 281.

Simon Dyson posted a 70 and was England's leader.

Martin Kaymer came in with 34 for his 73.

Starting with two bogeys, Steve Stricker had a 71.

Had Clarke caught any of the golf on the television before preparing for his own tee-time, it would have been Garcia who might have caught his attention. Starting the day at four over par, nine shots behind, the Spaniard was always too far back to worry the leader, but his superb start showed that even the worst of the British summer weather could not hinder anyone playing terrific golf. Garcia birdied four of the first seven holes to get back to level, having holed an 80-footer from the front of the green for a 3 at the fourth. Mickelson, a couple of hours later, was the only other player to make a birdie at the fearsome hole over the weekend.

A double-bogey at the eighth, after he drove into a gully in the right rough, put the brakes on a really low round, but two birdies in the last three holes meant a 68 for Garcia and he finished tied

Davis Love III (right) had a 72 to secure a top-10 place.

In the Words of the
of the
Competitors…

"The rain fortunately hasn't been too long. They've been little squalls that have been coming through here. It really hasn't been too bad, and you can tell by the scores that guys are dealing with it pretty well."

—Steve Stricker

"The Open this week has been amazing for me."

—Tom Lewis

"It was brutal out there. I think I held up pretty well. I hung in there all day, made some birdies on the back to get in there, and just unfortunately made the double-bogey on 14, which really took all my momentum out."

—Dustin Johnson

"I love playing links golf because I'm able to show a little bit of my game and hit some shots around the course that I don't get to hit in the States a whole lot. It's fun for me to be able to use my imagination and play the game a little bit differently and how it's meant to be played over here."

—Rickie Fowler

"I put myself in position and hit it well enough to finish better than (57th)."

—Ricky Barnes

Excerpts FROM THE Press

New US Open Champion Rory McIlroy had a disappointing weekend, with 74 and 73.

for ninth place at two over. That meant he would be exempt for the 2012 Open, whereas he had only qualified for the 2011 Championship just a fortnight beforehand when it looked as if his run of Major appearances dating back to the 1999 Open would come to an end. After he finished tied for seventh at the US Open, following a couple of lean years, it was good to see the Spaniard back in contention and smiling again.

His playing partner was not so chuffed. McIlroy, who was penalised a shot when his ball moved on the seventh green after he had addressed it, closed with a 73 to be seven over but gave vent to his frustrations at the weather. "It's been a tough week for me," said

Sharing the day's low score with a 68, Sergio Garcia finished on 282 to tie for ninth place.

Sergio Garcia's Revival

'Playing The Open Always Very Special'

Resurgence became the catchword of the 140th Open Championship. Darren Clarke was at the top of the leaderboard, seemingly years past his prime. Thomas Bjorn was playing as if it were 2003 all over again, the Americans were charging, and a Spaniard was back in contention in the game's oldest Major.

The R&A made sure the spirit of Seve Ballesteros was very much in evidence at Royal St George's. Tributes to the three-time Open Champion were all round the golf course. Maybe that's what spurred Sergio Garcia to play so well over the Sandwich links.

For most of the season it looked as if Garcia wouldn't be at Royal St George's, a strange situation for a man with seven top-10s in The Open, including runner-up in 2007. Garcia's chances of competing looked slim when he had to withdraw from International Final Qualifying with a finger injury. However, the Spaniard rediscovered his game just in time. He finished seventh in the US Open and lost

in a playoff to Pablo Larrazabal in the BMW International Open in Munich.

Garcia's playoff loss had a silver lining. It earned him a late ticket to Sandwich through a mini-money list that concluded with the Munich tournament.

"Even though I was disappointed with not winning the BMW in Munich, there was something that made me smile a little bit, which was that I knew that I was going to come here to Royal St George's and play The Open, which was always very special," Garcia said.

He seized his opportunity with both hands and held on tightly for a roller coaster ride over the Sandwich links.

Out two and a half hours before the leaders in the final round alongside Rory McIlroy, Garcia quickly lit up the leaderboard with four birdies in seven holes. That moved him to level par from four over at the start of the final round. He was just five off Clarke's lead and in position to put pressure on the Northern Irishman.

"Sometimes you feel so in control and

sometimes it feels like everything goes wrong," Garcia said. "That's the beauty about this game, that it can be so giving and at the same time it can be so annoying."

Garcia proved that statement true with the way he played the tough, par-4 eighth hole. A bad drive cost him a double-bogey and stopped his momentum. "The funniest thing about it is I didn't play eight that badly and I made double. That's what can happen here," he said.

Bogeys at the 13th and 17th holes were offset by birdies at the 16th and 18th as the Spaniard posted a 2-under-par 68 to finish tied for ninth.

"Me and my playing partner, we've played in the worst of weather throughout the week with the draw we had, and you can't be disappointed about the week then," he said.

Mark down the 140th Open as another step in the resurgence of Sergio Garcia.

— Alistair Tait

Round of the **Day**

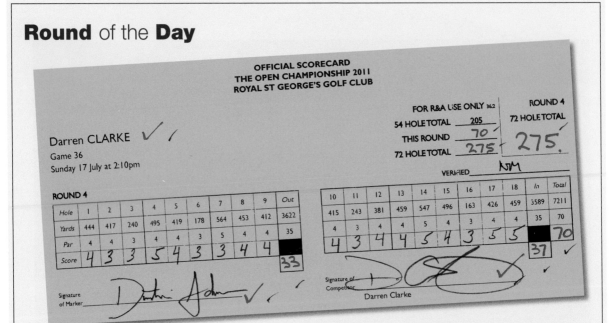

OFFICIAL SCORECARD
THE OPEN CHAMPIONSHIP 2011
ROYAL ST GEORGE'S GOLF CLUB

Darren CLARKE ✓ ✓
Game 36
Sunday 17 July at 2:10pm

FOR R&A USE ONLY 362
54 HOLE TOTAL   205
THIS ROUND   70
72 HOLE TOTAL   275

ROUND 4
72 HOLE TOTAL
275.

VERIFIED   NM

ROUND 4

Hole	1	2	3	4	5	6	7	8	9	Out	10	11	12	13	14	15	16	17	18	In	Total
Yards	444	417	240	495	419	178	564	453	412	3622	415	243	381	459	547	496	163	426	459	3589	7211
Par	4	4	3	4	4	3	5	4	4	35	4	3	4	4	5	4	3	4	4	35	70
Score	4	3	3	5	4	3	3	4	4	33	4	3	4	4	5	4	3	5	5	37	70

Signature of Marker

Signature of Competitor   Darren Clarke

Darren Clarke's play was so steady in the fourth round that he could afford bogeys on the last two holes and still win by three strokes with his level-par 70 and aggregate of 275, five under par.

Clarke scored a birdie at the second hole with a sand wedge to four feet, gave that shot back at the fourth, then posted an eagle-3 on the seventh with an 8-iron from 198 yards and a 16-foot putt. He made pars on the next nine holes until the 17th.

Just when did Clarke begin to think that it was his day?

"You never really think that until you're on the 18th green with a couple of shots ahead. You never know what is going to happen," Clarke said. "I got a couple of good breaks that went my way. Yesterday I played as well as I could from tee to green and I didn't really get anything out of it. Today I played not bad. I played okay. I got a couple of good breaks that went my way. Also at the same time I hit lots of great putts which burnt the edges and didn't go in. So it sort of balanced out.

"I did not take anything for granted. On 17 I was not going to make anything worse than bogey. I was trying to play the last two holes pretty smart, and I hit a really good shot off the 18th tee right in the middle of the fairway."

Fourth Round Scores	
Players Under Par	**6**
Players At Par	**5**
Players Over Par	**60**

Clarke said: 'On 17 I was not going to make anything worse than bogey.'

YE Yang's 72 included four bogeys.

Fredrik Jacobson, with a 72, took bogey at the last.

the US Open Champion. "I felt I did well the first couple of rounds, but I struggled a bit in the bad weather at the weekend."

He added: "I'm not a fan of golf tournaments where the outcome is predicted so much by the weather. It's not my sort of golf. I'm disappointed with the way I finished, obviously, but I'll just have to wait until next year to try and make a good run at this tournament. But there is no point in changing your game for one week a year."

Despite admitting that his success on links courses in the past had come when the conditions were calm, McIlroy won the Silver Medal as the leading amateur in 2007 at Carnoustie. His successor this year was Tom Lewis, another youngster with a bright future. He hung on to finish at nine over and three strokes ahead of the US Amateur Champion Peter Uihlein, his only other rival for the Silver Medal. Lewis had scores of 74, 76, and 74 to follow his record 65 in the first round, and any brief thoughts of turning professional immediately were

Lucas Glover slipped back on 73 and 74.

"

"Oh, man, that was some of the most fun I've had competitively. It was really a fun start, and it was exciting…. And then, later on when I ended up missing, I hit great putts that caught the lip or looked like they were going in. It was a fun day."

—Phil Mickelson

"These young people are just what I was … mere babes with passion and dreams that maybe some-day we can be a Jack Nicklaus, and that's what I had."

—Tom Watson

"I struggled on the front nine. I was four over after nine holes, and I just tried to keep it together. That was my goal to shoot under par on the back nine…. Overall, it was an okay week."

—Martin Kaymer

"It was nice to be in the mix, for sure. But at the same time you want to have a chance to win with about three, four holes to go, and I didn't really do that. But that was all I had this week, and it's a really positive step for me."

—Anthony Kim

"

Webb Simpson returned a 73 for 285.

Richard Green's 71 yielded a tie for 16th.

Charl Schwartzel posted a 34-38–72.

discarded. Instead, the 20-year-old was looking forward to facing Uihlein and the Americans in the Walker Cup at Royal Aberdeen in September.

Given how most of the players seemed to play the Sandwich links as if undertaking an exploratory expedition, perhaps it was fitting that it was Lewis and Clarke picking up the Medals at the end of the week. However, Lewis noted how he had finished below his namesake and playing partner for the first two rounds, Tom Watson, who was a highly creditable tied for 26th on six over. And after playing with Mickelson on Saturday, Lewis did not feel he was ready to join the professionals just yet. "I've got things to learn, as I've just lost by about 20 shots this week," he said. "Playing with Phil yesterday made me feel terrible around the greens. If you are going to play with the best players in the world, you have to chip and putt like they do."

Lewis has high standards but he should not be too hard on himself. Few players can compare their short games with that of Mickelson and not come off unfavourably. When it comes to producing a brilliant burst of scoring, Mickelson remains capable of the most dramatic

Leaning Towards Links Success

If Phil Mickelson thought he could persuade himself and everyone else he could be a competitor in The Open Championship, well Phil certainly became a believer. By the first nine of the fourth round, others joined him.

The Mickelson strategy was unique. He came to Royal St George's telling everyone to ignore history. Only once in 17 previous attempts, a tie for third at Royal Troon in 2004, had the man they call Lefty finished in the top 10 in The Open. When the tournament was last held at Royal St George's in 2003, he tied for a mediocre 59th.

Mickelson hit the ball high, said the critics, making him vulnerable on Open courses, where the wind whistled and the fairways were full of bad bounces.

"I'm not trying to fix any past poor play," Mickelson insisted two days before the first shot was struck. "I'm trying to come here and play the way links golf should be played … I actually really enjoy it."

Five shots behind Darren Clarke after 54 holes, the 41-year-old Mickelson, battling the storm, went five under par for the day and into a tie with Clarke after Phil had an eagle-3 on the par-5 seventh hole.

That Clarke also would eagle the same hole and eventually go on to win his first Major, didn't diminish Mickelson's joy. He returned a 30-38—68 and tied Dustin Johnson for second place at two-under 278, three shots back of Clarke's 275.

"I was having a lot of fun," was the Mickelson comment, "the most fun I've had."

In fact, two days earlier he said he wanted nasty weather, and he got what he wished, disproving any theory he didn't have a chance in difficult conditions.

"I was just hitting the shot I was seeing every time, and the ball was rolling where I was wanting it," Mickelson said. "I hit some of the best shots I've hit in the wind. Not just today, but all week. I made some great putts, and then later on I ended up missing them."

At the 11th, he failed to hole a par putt estimated around two feet. He couldn't recover. There would be no fifth Major title added to his resumé.

Mickelson said when he realized Clarke wasn't making mistakes he would have to force the issue, trying himself to make birdies. As so often happens in that situation, he made bogeys instead.

He was magnanimous towards Clarke, who had called Phil two years earlier with advice and support when Amy Mickelson, his wife, was diagnosed with breast cancer.

"He's a tremendous person and a very good friend," Mickelson said of Clarke. "And I couldn't be happier for him. It was fun to try and make a run at him."

—**Art Spander**

Championship Hole Summary

HOLE	PAR	YARDS	EAGLES	BIRDIES	PARS	BOGEYS	D.BOGEYS	HIGHER	RANK	AVERAGE
1	4	444	0	24	313	110	6	0	8	4.22
2	4	417	0	58	315	75	5	0	16	4.06
3	3	240	0	34	281	130	8	0	6	3.25
4	4	495	0	16	227	177	26	7	1	4.52
5	4	419	0	51	309	89	2	2	12	4.11
6	3	178	1	40	292	106	10	4	9	3.21
7	5	564	19	202	192	38	2	0	18	4.56
8	4	453	0	33	251	140	27	2	2	4.37
9	4	412	1	40	280	117	12	3	7	4.24
OUT	**35**	**3,622**	**21**	**498**	**2,460**	**982**	**98**	**18**		**36.54**
10	4	415	0	53	275	112	13	0	11	4.19
11	3	243	0	34	279	132	8	0	5	3.25
12	4	381	0	79	300	70	4	0	17	4.00
13	4	459	0	60	291	95	6	1	12	4.11
14	5	547	1	105	256	61	19	11	15	5.07
15	4	496	0	31	284	124	13	1	4	4.27
16	3	163	1	54	316	76	6	0	14	3.07
17	4	426	0	48	276	120	9	0	10	4.20
18	4	459	0	32	256	151	14	0	3	4.32
IN	**35**	**3,589**	**2**	**496**	**2,533**	**941**	**92**	**13**		**36.48**
TOTAL	**70**	**7,211**	**23**	**994**	**4,993**	**1,923**	**190**	**31**		**73.02**

Championship Totals	
Rounds Under Par	66
Rounds At Par	43
Rounds Over Par	344

Anders Hansen fell with a 76.

explosions. Here was another example. He holed from 15 feet at the second and then birdied the fourth and the sixth. At the par-5 seventh he had a 50-footer for his eagle and drained that as well. Five under for the day, he was now tied for the lead with Clarke.

The leader had started uncertainly by pulling his opening drive into the rough and then leaving his long approach putt 13 feet short. When the par putt went in it was a great settler, and then he hit a sand wedge to four feet at the second and made what would turn out to be his only birdie of the day. He led Johnson by two and the gap was extended to three when the American bogeyed the short third.

Clarke had holed a good par putt at the third, but missed from eight feet at the fourth, so fell back to five under. Mickelson joined him at five under, but when Clarke got to the seventh he hit an 8-iron to 16 feet and holed for the eagle. At seven under, he was now two ahead again, but Mickelson, after missing a chance at the ninth, holed a 30-footer at the 10th to get to six under. He had covered the first 10 holes in 33 strokes.

But then Mickelson had an aberration on the 11th green and missed

Tom Lehman returned a 75 and tied for 22nd place.

Tom Watson finished on 286.

his tap-in putt from two feet. "It was just a dumb mental error," he said. It also proved to be the first of four bogeys in six holes. The birdies had dried up and he had to settle for a 68 to finish at two under par. "Oh man, that was some of the most fun I've had competitively," Mickelson said. "It was fun to try and make a run. But when I saw Darren wasn't going to make a mistake, I had to start trying to make birdies and that's when I ended up making a couple of bogeys." His runner-up status bettered his previous Open best of third at Royal Troon in 2004.

Clarke was safely making pars until the 11th, where he found a bunker. He came out to seven feet and holed that for another par. The danger man now was Johnson. His power was enormous, but it could not help him at the 419-yard fifth, where he drove over the mounds and through the green but could not get up and down for a birdie. Worse, he dropped his second shot of the day at the sixth, although he was able to reclaim it at the seventh. It was his birdies at the 10th and 12th holes that took him within two strokes of Clarke and back into contention.

They arrived at the dangerous 14th with the Claret Jug at stake. Even the strongest men have cracked in this far corner of the course, Bernhard Langer coming to mind, and when Johnson's 2-iron second shot curved to the right and out of bounds, it was a fatal blow to

Watson's Visit To Normandy

At the finish Tom Watson revealed that on his way to The Open, he had taken a side trip to France's Normandy coast, where on 6 June 1944 was the largest amphibious invasion in modern history.

"I visited the British military grave site at Ranville first and then I went on to Sword Beach, which was the eastern flank, and then we overnighted in Caen, and then the next day we went to the US cemetery and Pointe du Hoc and Omaha Beach," Watson said. "It was very emotional.

"I wanted to see, first of all, Pointe du Hoc. It was man against man and gun against gun. Talk about a disadvantage. It was like me playing Phil Mickelson on this golf course. The Rangers, the Second Battalion Rangers, had to go up 115 feet in the air, straight up, and the Germans were up there shooting at them. And they managed to do it.

"To see the cemetery there and the 9,000-plus marble crosses is a striking reminder of what the human condition can do."

4

Excerpts
FROM THE Press

"The smile remained fixed on Phil Mickelson's face long after the circumstances of the day should have wiped it off."

—**Tim Dahlberg,** *The Associated Press*

"The irony won't be lost on Darren Clarke, a man who always seemed to be in a hurry. Clarke's first Major title — in his 20th appearance in The Open — has come towards the back end of an honour-laden career."

—**Philip Reid,** *The Irish Times*

"This was Ireland's sixth Major title in four years and an astounding third for the wonderful 'Wee North' in just 13 months … yet this triumph by Darren Clarke must warm the heart of every golfer on the planet."

—**Karl MacGinty,** *Irish Independent*

"Darren Clarke arrived at Royal St George's last week as a 200-to-1 outsider to win the 140th Open Championship and left it as a Major Champion with the world at his feet."

—**Peter Dixon,** *The Times*

"Sergio Garcia heads for his 50th consecutive Major appearance next month in a positive mood after a final-round 68 at Royal St George's."

—**Neil Squires,** *Daily Express*

"Darren Clarke's win was such a shock, he originally was planning to commentate the final two days at The Open."

—**James Nursey,** *Daily Mirror*

Simon Kahn advanced 21 places.

Adam Scott's 75 tied for 25th.

Spencer Levin's last three: 69, 81, 69.

Ryan Moore went from 76 to 69.

'They were sensational for me all week,' Clarke said of the spectators. 'They were out there roaring and shouting.'

his chances. He ended up with a double-bogey-7, and Clarke, who safely collected his par, was now four ahead.

"You don't get many opportunities to make birdie and it was definitely a go situation," Johnson said. "But if I had to do it over again, I'd hit a 3-wood instead of a 2-iron." It was the third time in six Majors that Johnson had played in the final pairing on the last day, but the breaks had yet to go his way. He bogeyed the last to drop into a tie for second with Mickelson. "It was brutal out there and I think I held up pretty well," he added. "I hung in there all day and made some birdies on the back to get back in there, but unfortunately the double-bogey on 14 took all my momentum out."

Clarke had his moments of good fortune, skirting

the cross bunkers on the 15th as he had on the ninth, but the pars kept on coming until three-putts from the front of the 17th green and from the back left of the last green. Even in his moment of triumph, Clarke was concerned with trying to get the crowd to quieten down for Johnson to be able to finish. "That's etiquette, that's manners, that's politeness, that's the way the game should be played," Clarke said. "The crowd was just getting a little bit over exuberant."

It was a gesture to a fellow player that was typical of the man. Having started the week ranked 111th in the world and rated a 200-1 chance by the bookmakers, he finished it looking every inch an Open Champion. "I have to admit Darren wasn't on my list of likely winners at the start of the week, and

Edward Demery, captain of Royal St George's, handed Clarke the Claret Jug.

Tom Lewis received the Silver Medal.

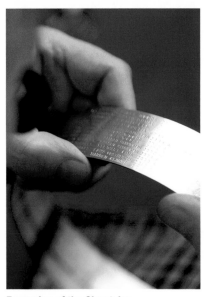

Engraving of the Claret Jug.

I don't think he was on anyone's probably, although he had been playing some very good golf recently," reflected Peter Dawson, the Chief Executive of The R&A. "But as it became increasingly possible that he was going to win, I got increasingly the feeling that this was a Champion we really wanted to have, given his history of the game and everything he's done for golf. He is just the right stature to be Open Champion. We couldn't be more delighted."

"To get my name on this thing," Clarke said, nodding at the Claret Jug in front of him, "means more than anything. But what's more important is when I get home later today and my boys have the trophy in their hands and look at their dad's name on the trophy." The following day, Clarke presented his Gold Medal to Royal Portrush to sit in the trophy cabinet alongside that of Fred Daly from 1947. He wanted everyone visiting the club to be able to see it.

Apparently Tyrone and Conor, who spent the weekend playing in the morning and watching their father on television in the afternoon, had been looking at Daly's Medal the week before The Open. The story had gone round that an assistant professional had told them: "Your dad has not got his hands on one of them just yet."

He has now.

ANOTHER POPULAR CHAMPION

By John Hopkins

There is something about the turbulent links of Royal St George's that ensures that many a winner of The Open Championship is a popular character whose victory strikes a chord not just inside the golfing community but outside it as well. Think of Sandy Lyle in 1985, the first British Champion since Tony Jacklin in 1969, and of how a spectator, seeing Bernhard Langer putting on the 72nd green with a chance to deny Lyle, shouted out: "Don't you dare." Think of Henry Cotton in 1934, leading by 10 strokes after three rounds on his way to becoming the first British-born Open Champion for 11 years.

And now think of Darren Clarke as he won The Open at his 20th attempt, more than any other first-time winner, and, at 42, becoming the oldest winner since Robert de Vicenzo at Hoylake in 1967 at the age of 44. Think of Clarke's sturdy build, his iron grey hair peeping out from above his visor, and the powerful force he generated with his irons. Clarke's swing resembles what John Jacobs once described as "two turns and a swish" in its simplicity and repetitiousness. He hits down so hard with his irons that, while the earth does not tremble, you fear for the ball. Think of the broad smile that appeared to be glued to his face for much of the week and of his brisk, straight-backed walk, which seems a physical manifestation of his brisk, no-nonsense way of speaking.

In the months leading up to Sandwich, Clarke had been playing poorly. The harder he practised — and Clarke practises very hard — the worse he got, seemingly. Rounds of 81 and 75 at a tournament in Morocco in the spring were so far below his own standards that he contemplated giving up the game. This might have been a relief from the torment he was going through on the golf course but was hardly what his accountant would have recommended. At that time, Clarke's outgoings were exceeding his income.

Clarke was advised by Andrew "Chubby" Chandler, his manager, to take a holiday. It made all the difference. Clarke went to the Bahamas for three weeks and won his first tournament after his return. There is an echo here of Cotton nearly 80 years earlier. Cotton arrived at Sandwich in a state of desperation, bringing four sets of clubs with him and "unable to hit his hat with any of them," according to the late Henry Longhurst. He took a day off before the Championship, caddied for his wife, and that break in his routine was the making of him.

Of his peers, Clarke always seemed the one most likely to win an Open because of his technique. Other golfers are at home on inland courses with holes lined by beech, oak, and pine trees and scarcely a breath of wind to disturb them. Clarke's physique could have been designed to help him battle a links course, to wrestle it to the ground and stamp on it. You need only to look at the width of his stance, the brevity of his swing, the firmness of stroke to realise that here is a man who grew up hitting into a wind, whether from the side of a 20-foot-high sand dune or the springy turf of a links.

Again and again Clarke gave a demonstration of just how magnificent ball-striking can neutralise the perils of a course as difficult as Royal St George's in predominantly beastly conditions: He cut a 7-iron to bring it in on a daring line so that it landed perhaps six feet beyond a sentinel bunker on the right of the 18th green on Friday; he

hit a magnificent long iron through the wind to within a handspan of the flag on the ridged, tricky fourth green on Saturday; he thumped an 8-iron to the heart of the seventh green on Sunday to set up his second eagle in three days on that hole. All week long, Clarke was doing what he does best. Even his putting, not his strongest suit, was performing well.

It helped hugely that Clarke's personal life had entered a new, happier phase. Following the death from cancer of Heather, his first wife, in 2006, he was now engaged to be married to Alison Campbell, a former Miss Northern Ireland who ran a model agency in Belfast. He had moved himself and his two boys from Ascot in England to Portrush near Dungannon, his birthplace, where they came under the caring eye and filial rivalry of his sister and her two children.

That was one half of the trick that turned Clarke into the Open Champion. The other was a session on the eve of the Championship with Dr Bob Rotella, the sports psychologist with whom Clarke has had the longest relationship. "Dr Bob and I worked on my putting," Clarke said without revealing further details.

They worked on his state of mind, too. "Darren had been getting more and more frustrated," Rotella said. "He got tied up in knots. I told him I just wanted him to look at where he wanted to hit it and hit it. He had the skills. It was a question of unfreezing them. A top athlete's mind is very quiet, and I knew Darren had peace of mind. I told him, 'You are unstoppable if you are unflappable, and if you let it happen, it will be party time.'"

He was and it did. All week long there was an unusual calm about him. He was a long way from the fiery player of earlier years who might follow a careless three-putt with a silly double-bogey. Having rediscovered a serenity in his private life, he had found the form necessary to win the one trophy he coveted more than any other.

The Open Championship Results

Year	Champion	Score	Margin	Runners-up	Venue
1860	Willie Park Sr	174	2	Tom Morris Sr	Prestwick
1861	Tom Morris Sr	163	4	Willie Park Sr	Prestwick
1862	Tom Morris Sr	163	13	Willie Park Sr	Prestwick
1863	Willie Park Sr	168	2	Tom Morris Sr	Prestwick
1864	Tom Morris Sr	167	2	Andrew Strath	Prestwick
1865	Andrew Strath	162	2	Willie Park Sr	Prestwick
1866	Willie Park Sr	169	2	David Park	Prestwick
1867	Tom Morris Sr	170	2	Willie Park Sr	Prestwick
1868	Tommy Morris Jr	154	3	Tom Morris Sr	Prestwick
1869	Tommy Morris Jr	157	11	Bob Kirk	Prestwick
1870	Tommy Morris Jr	149	12	Bob Kirk, Davie Strath	Prestwick
1871	*No Competition*				
1872	Tommy Morris Jr	166	3	Davie Strath	Prestwick
1873	Tom Kidd	179	1	Jamie Anderson	St Andrews
1874	Mungo Park	159	2	Tommy Morris Jr	Musselburgh
1875	Willie Park Sr	166	2	Bob Martin	Prestwick
1876	Bob Martin	176	—	Davie Strath	St Andrews
	(Martin was awarded the title when Strath refused to play-off)				
1877	Jamie Anderson	160	2	Bob Pringle	Musselburgh
1878	Jamie Anderson	157	2	Bob Kirk	Prestwick
1879	Jamie Anderson	169	3	Jamie Allan, Andrew Kirkaldy	St Andrews
1880	Bob Ferguson	162	5	Peter Paxton	Musselburgh
1881	Bob Ferguson	170	3	Jamie Anderson	Prestwick
1882	Bob Ferguson	171	3	Willie Fernie	St Andrews
1883	Willie Fernie	158	Playoff	Bob Ferguson	Musselburgh
1884	Jack Simpson	160	4	Douglas Rolland, Willie Fernie	Prestwick
1885	Bob Martin	171	1	Archie Simpson	St Andrews
1886	David Brown	157	2	Willie Campbell	Musselburgh
1887	Willie Park Jr	161	1	Bob Martin	Prestwick
1888	Jack Burns	171	1	David Anderson Jr, Ben Sayers	St Andrews
1889	Willie Park Jr	155	Playoff	Andrew Kirkaldy	Musselburgh
1890	John Ball Jr*	164	3	Willie Fernie, Archie Simpson	Prestwick
1891	Hugh Kirkaldy	166	2	Willie Fernie, Andrew Kirkaldy	St Andrews
	(From 1892 the competition was extended to 72 holes)				
1892	Harold Hilton*	305	3	John Ball Jr*, Hugh Kirkaldy, Sandy Herd	Muirfield

Ernie Els (2002)

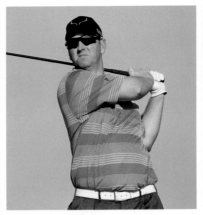
David Duval (2001)

John Daly (1995)

Year	Champion	Score	Margin	Runners-up	Venue
1893	Willie Auchterlonie	322	2	John Laidlay*	Prestwick
1894	JH Taylor	326	5	Douglas Rolland	St George's
1895	JH Taylor	322	4	Sandy Herd	St Andrews
1896	Harry Vardon	316	Playoff	JH Taylor	Muirfield
1897	Harold Hilton*	314	1	James Braid	Royal Liverpool
1898	Harry Vardon	307	1	Willie Park Jr	Prestwick
1899	Harry Vardon	310	5	Jack White	St George's
1900	JH Taylor	309	8	Harry Vardon	St Andrews
1901	James Braid	309	3	Harry Vardon	Muirfield
1902	Sandy Herd	307	1	Harry Vardon, James Braid	Royal Liverpool
1903	Harry Vardon	300	6	Tom Vardon	Prestwick
1904	Jack White	296	1	James Braid, JH Taylor	Royal St George's
1905	James Braid	318	5	JH Taylor, Rowland Jones	St Andrews
1906	James Braid	300	4	JH Taylor	Muirfield
1907	Arnaud Massy	312	2	JH Taylor	Royal Liverpool
1908	James Braid	291	8	Tom Ball	Prestwick
1909	JH Taylor	295	6	James Braid, Tom Ball	Cinque Ports
1910	James Braid	299	4	Sandy Herd	St Andrews
1911	Harry Vardon	303	Playoff	Arnaud Massy	Royal St George's
1912	Ted Ray	295	4	Harry Vardon	Muirfield
1913	JH Taylor	304	8	Ted Ray	Royal Liverpool
1914	Harry Vardon	306	3	JH Taylor	Prestwick
1915-1919	*No Championship*				
1920	George Duncan	303	2	Sandy Herd	Cinque Ports
1921	Jock Hutchison	296	Playoff	Roger Wethered*	St Andrews
1922	Walter Hagen	300	1	George Duncan, Jim Barnes	Royal St George's
1923	Arthur Havers	295	1	Walter Hagen	Troon
1924	Walter Hagen	301	1	Ernest Whitcombe	Royal Liverpool
1925	Jim Barnes	300	1	Archie Compston, Ted Ray	Prestwick
1926	Bobby Jones*	291	2	Al Watrous	Royal Lytham
1927	Bobby Jones*	285	6	Aubrey Boomer, Fred Robson	St Andrews
1928	Walter Hagen	292	2	Gene Sarazen	Royal St George's
1929	Walter Hagen	292	6	Johnny Farrell	Muirfield
1930	Bobby Jones*	291	2	Leo Diegel, Macdonald Smith	Royal Liverpool
1931	Tommy Armour	296	1	Jose Jurado	Carnoustie
1932	Gene Sarazen	283	5	Macdonald Smith	Prince's
1933	Denny Shute	292	Playoff	Craig Wood	St Andrews

Todd Hamilton (2004)

Mark Calcavecchia (1989)

Mark O'Meara (1998)

Year	Champion	Score	Margin	Runners-up	Venue
1934	Henry Cotton	283	5	Sid Brews	Royal St George's
1935	Alf Perry	283	4	Alf Padgham	Muirfield
1936	Alf Padgham	287	1	Jimmy Adams	Royal Liverpool
1937	Henry Cotton	290	2	Reg Whitcombe	Carnoustie
1938	Reg Whitcombe	295	2	Jimmy Adams	Royal St George's
1939	Dick Burton	290	2	Johnny Bulla	St Andrews
1940-1945 *No Championship*					
1946	Sam Snead	290	4	Bobby Locke, Johnny Bulla	St Andrews
1947	Fred Daly	293	1	Reg Horne, Frank Stranahan*	Royal Liverpool
1948	Henry Cotton	284	5	Fred Daly	Muirfield
1949	Bobby Locke	283	Playoff	Harry Bradshaw	Royal St George's
1950	Bobby Locke	279	2	Roberto de Vicenzo	Troon
1951	Max Faulkner	285	2	Antonio Cerda	Royal Portrush
1952	Bobby Locke	287	1	Peter Thomson	Royal Lytham
1953	Ben Hogan	282	4	Frank Stranahan*, Dai Rees, Peter Thomson, Antonio Cerda	Carnoustie
1954	Peter Thomson	283	1	Syd Scott, Dai Rees, Bobby Locke	Royal Birkdale
1955	Peter Thomson	281	2	John Fallon	St Andrews
1956	Peter Thomson	286	3	Flory Van Donck	Royal Liverpool
1957	Bobby Locke	279	3	Peter Thomson	St Andrews
1958	Peter Thomson	278	Playoff	Dave Thomas	Royal Lytham
1959	Gary Player	284	2	Flory van Donck, Fred Bullock	Muirfield
1960	Kel Nagle	278	1	Arnold Palmer	St Andrews
1961	Arnold Palmer	284	1	Dai Rees	Royal Birkdale
1962	Arnold Palmer	276	6	Kel Nagle	Troon
1963	Bob Charles	277	Playoff	Phil Rodgers	Royal Lytham
1964	Tony Lema	279	5	Jack Nicklaus	St Andrews
1965	Peter Thomson	285	2	Christy O'Connor Sr, Brian Huggett	Royal Birkdale
1966	Jack Nicklaus	282	1	Dave Thomas, Doug Sanders	Muirfield
1967	Roberto de Vicenzo	278	2	Jack Nicklaus	Royal Liverpool
1968	Gary Player	289	2	Jack Nicklaus, Bob Charles	Carnoustie
1969	Tony Jacklin	280	2	Bob Charles	Royal Lytham
1970	Jack Nicklaus	283	Playoff	Doug Sanders	St Andrews
1971	Lee Trevino	278	1	Liang Huan Lu	Royal Birkdale
1972	Lee Trevino	278	1	Jack Nicklaus	Muirfield
1973	Tom Weiskopf	276	3	Neil Coles, Johnny Miller	Troon
1974	Gary Player	282	4	Peter Oosterhuis	Royal Lytham
1975	Tom Watson	279	Playoff	Jack Newton	Carnoustie
1976	Johnny Miller	279	6	Jack Nicklaus, Seve Ballesteros	Royal Birkdale

Year	Champion	Score	Margin	Runners-up	Venue
1977	Tom Watson	268	1	Jack Nicklaus	Turnberry
1978	Jack Nicklaus	281	2	Simon Owen, Ben Crenshaw, Ray Floyd, Tom Kite	St Andrews
1979	Seve Ballesteros	283	3	Jack Nicklaus, Ben Crenshaw	Royal Lytham
1980	Tom Watson	271	4	Lee Trevino	Muirfield
1981	Bill Rogers	276	4	Bernhard Langer	Royal St George's
1982	Tom Watson	284	1	Peter Oosterhuis, Nick Price	Royal Troon
1983	Tom Watson	275	1	Hale Irwin, Andy Bean	Royal Birkdale
1984	Seve Ballesteros	276	2	Bernhard Langer, Tom Watson	St Andrews
1985	Sandy Lyle	282	1	Payne Stewart	Royal St George's
1986	Greg Norman	280	5	Gordon J Brand	Turnberry
1987	Nick Faldo	279	1	Rodger Davis, Paul Azinger	Muirfield
1988	Seve Ballesteros	273	2	Nick Price	Royal Lytham
1989	Mark Calcavecchia	275	Playoff	Greg Norman, Wayne Grady	Royal Troon
1990	Nick Faldo	270	5	Mark McNulty, Payne Stewart	St Andrews
1991	Ian Baker-Finch	272	2	Mike Harwood	Royal Birkdale
1992	Nick Faldo	272	1	John Cook	Muirfield
1993	Greg Norman	267	2	Nick Faldo	Royal St George's
1994	Nick Price	268	1	Jesper Parnevik	Turnberry
1995	John Daly	282	Playoff	Costantino Rocca	St Andrews
1996	Tom Lehman	271	2	Mark McCumber, Ernie Els	Royal Lytham
1997	Justin Leonard	272	3	Jesper Parnevik, Darren Clarke	Royal Troon
1998	Mark O'Meara	280	Playoff	Brian Watts	Royal Birkdale
1999	Paul Lawrie	290	Playoff	Justin Leonard, Jean Van de Velde	Carnoustie
2000	Tiger Woods	269	8	Ernie Els, Thomas Bjorn	St Andrews
2001	David Duval	274	3	Niclas Fasth	Royal Lytham
2002	Ernie Els	278	Playoff	Thomas Levet, Stuart Appleby, Steve Elkington	Muirfield
2003	Ben Curtis	283	1	Thomas Bjorn, Vijay Singh	Royal St George's
2004	Todd Hamilton	274	Playoff	Ernie Els	Royal Troon
2005	Tiger Woods	274	5	Colin Montgomerie	St Andrews
2006	Tiger Woods	270	2	Chris DiMarco	Royal Liverpool
2007	Padraig Harrington	277	Playoff	Sergio Garcia	Carnoustie
2008	Padraig Harrington	283	4	Ian Poulter	Royal Birkdale
2009	Stewart Cink	278	Playoff	Tom Watson	Turnberry
2010	Louis Oosthuizen	272	7	Lee Westwood	St Andrews
2011	Darren Clarke	275	3	Phil Mickelson, Dustin Johnson	Royal St George's

*Denotes amateurs

Paul Lawrie (1999)

Tom Watson (1975, 1977, 1980, 1982, 1983)

The Open Championship Records

Most Victories

6: Harry Vardon, 1896, 1898, 1899, 1903, 1911, 1914
5: James Braid, 1901, 1905, 1906, 1908, 1910; JH Taylor, 1894, 1895, 1900, 1909, 1913; Peter Thomson, 1954, 1955, 1956, 1958, 1965; Tom Watson, 1975, 1977, 1980, 1982, 1983

Most Runner-Up or Joint Runner-Up Finishes

7: Jack Nicklaus, 1964, 1967, 1968, 1972, 1976, 1977, 1979
6: JH Taylor, 1896, 1904, 1905, 1906, 1907, 1914

Oldest Winners

Tom Morris Sr, 1867, 46 years 99 days
Roberto de Vicenzo, 1967, 44 years 93 days
Harry Vardon, 1914, 44 years 41 days

Youngest Winners

Tommy Morris Jr, 1868, 17 years 5 months 3 days
Willie Auchterlonie, 1893, 21 years 24 days
Seve Ballesteros, 1979, 22 years 3 months 12 days

Known Oldest and Youngest Competitors

74 years, 11 months, 24 days: Tom Morris Sr, 1896
74 years, 4 months, 9 days: Gene Sarazen, 1976
14 years, 4 months, 25 days: Tommy Morris Jr, 1865

Largest Margin of Victory

13 strokes, Tom Morris Sr, 1862
12 strokes, Tommy Morris Jr, 1870
11 strokes, Tommy Morris Jr, 1869
8 strokes, JH Taylor, 1900 and 1913; James Braid, 1908; Tiger Woods, 2000

Lowest Winning Total by a Champion

267, Greg Norman, Royal St George's 1993 – 66, 68, 69, 64
268, Tom Watson, Turnberry, 1977 – 69, 66, 67, 66; Nick Price, Turnberry, 1994 – 69, 66, 67, 66
269, Tiger Woods, St Andrews, 2000 – 67, 66, 67, 69

Lowest Total in Relation to Par Since 1963

19 under par: Tiger Woods, St Andrews, 2000 (269)
18 under par: Nick Faldo, St Andrews, 1990 (270); Tiger Woods, Royal Liverpool, 2006 (270)

Lowest Total by a Runner-Up

269: Jack Nicklaus, Turnberry, 1977 – 68, 70, 65, 66; Nick Faldo, Royal St George's, 1993 – 69, 63, 70, 67; Jesper Parnevik, Turnberry, 1994 – 68, 66, 68, 67

Lowest Total by an Amateur

281: Iain Pyman, Royal St George's, 1993 – 68, 72, 70, 71; Tiger Woods, Royal Lytham & St Annes, 1996 – 75, 66, 70, 70

Justin Leonard (1997)   **Ben Curtis (2003)**

Sandy Lyle (1985)

Lowest Individual Round

63: Mark Hayes, second round, Turnberry, 1977; Isao Aoki, third round, Muirfield, 1980; Greg Norman, second round, Turnberry, 1986; Paul Broadhurst, third round, St Andrews, 1990; Jodie Mudd, fourth round, Royal Birkdale, 1991; Nick Faldo, second round, Royal St George's, 1993; Payne Stewart, fourth round, Royal St George's, 1993; Rory McIlroy, first round, St Andrews, 2010

Lowest Individual Round by an Amateur

65: Tom Lewis, first round, Royal St George's, 2011

Lowest First Round

63: Rory McIlroy, St Andrews, 2010

Lowest Second Round

63: Mark Hayes, Turnberry, 1977; Greg Norman, Turnberry, 1986; Nick Faldo, Royal St George's, 1993

Lowest Third Round

63: Isao Aoki, Muirfield, 1980; Paul Broadhurst, St Andrews, 1990

Lowest Fourth Round

63: Jodie Mudd, Royal Birkdale, 1991; Payne Stewart, Royal St George's, 1993

Lowest Score over the First 36 Holes

130: Nick Faldo, Muirfield, 1992 – 66, 64

Lowest Score over the Middle 36 Holes

130: Fuzzy Zoeller, Turnberry, 1994 – 66, 64

Lowest Score over the Final 36 Holes

130: Tom Watson, Turnberry, 1977 – 65, 65; Ian Baker-Finch, Royal Birkdale, 1991 – 64, 66; Anders Forsbrand, Turnberry, 1994 – 66, 64

Lowest Score over the First 54 Holes

198: Tom Lehman, Royal Lytham & St Annes, 1996 – 67, 67, 64
199: Nick Faldo, St Andrews, 1990 – 67, 65, 67; Nick Faldo, Muirfield, 1992 – 66, 64, 69

Lowest Score over the Final 54 Holes

199: Nick Price, Turnberry, 1994 – 66, 67, 66

Lowest Score for Nine Holes

28: Denis Durnian, first nine, Royal Birkdale, 1983
29: Tom Haliburton, first nine, Royal Lytham & St Annes, 1963; Peter Thomson, first nine, Royal Lytham & St Annes, 1963; Tony Jacklin, first nine, St Andrews, 1970; Bill Longmuir, first nine, Royal Lytham & St Annes, 1979; David J Russell first nine, Royal Lytham & St Annes, 1988; Ian Baker-Finch, first nine, St Andrews, 1990; Paul Broadhurst, first nine, St Andrews, 1990; Ian Baker-Finch, first nine, Royal Birkdale, 1991; Paul McGinley, first nine, Royal Lytham & St Annes, 1996; Ernie Els, first nine, Muirfield, 2002; Sergio Garcia, first nine, Royal Liverpool, 2006

Most Successive Victories

4: Tommy Morris Jr, 1868-72 *(No Championship in 1871)*
3: Jamie Anderson, 1877-79; Bob Ferguson, 1880-82; Peter Thomson, 1954-56
2: Tom Morris Sr, 1861-62; JH Taylor, 1894-95; Harry Vardon, 1898-99; James Braid, 1905-06; Bobby Jones, 1926-27; Walter Hagen, 1928-29; Bobby Locke, 1949-50; Arnold Palmer, 1961-62; Lee Trevino, 1971-72; Tom Watson, 1982-83; Tiger Woods, 2005-06; Padraig Harrington, 2007-08

Amateurs Who Have Won The Open

3: Bobby Jones, Royal Lytham & St Annes, 1926; St Andrews, 1927; Royal Liverpool, 1930
2: Harold Hilton, Muirfield, 1892; Royal Liverpool, 1897
1: John Ball Jr, Prestwick, 1890

Champions Who Won on Debut

Willie Park Sr, Prestwick, 1860; Tom Kidd, St Andrews, 1873; Mungo Park, Musselburgh, 1874; Jock Hutchison, St Andrews, 1921; Denny Shute, St Andrews, 1933; Ben Hogan, Carnoustie, 1953; Tony Lema, St Andrews, 1964; Tom Watson, Carnoustie, 1975; Ben Curtis, Royal St George's, 2003

Greatest Interval Between First and Last Victory

19 years: JH Taylor, 1894-1913
18 years: Harry Vardon, 1896-1914
15 years: Willie Park Sr, 1860-75; Gary Player, 1959-74
14 years: Henry Cotton, 1934-48

Greatest Interval Between Victories

11 years: Henry Cotton, 1937-48 *(No Championship 1940-45)*
9 years: Willie Park Sr, 1866-75; Bob Martin, 1876-85; JH Taylor, 1900-09; Gary Player, 1959-68

Padraig Harrington (2007, 2008)

Champions Who Have Won in Three Separate Decades

Harry Vardon, 1896, 1898 & 1899/1903/1911 & 1914
JH Taylor, 1894 & 1895/1900 & 1909/1913
Gary Player, 1959, 1968, 1974

Competitors with the Most Top Five Finishes

16: JH Taylor; Jack Nicklaus

Competitors Who Have Recorded the Most Rounds Under Par From 1963

59: Jack Nicklaus
53: Nick Faldo

Competitors with the Most Finishes Under Par From 1963

14: Jack Nicklaus; Nick Faldo
13: Ernie Els; Tom Watson

Louis Oosthuizen (2010)

Tom Lehman (1996)

Champions Who Have Led Outright After Every Round

72 hole Championships
Ted Ray, 1912; Bobby Jones, 1927; Gene Sarazen, 1932; Henry Cotton, 1934; Tom Weiskopf, 1973; Tiger Woods, 2005
36 hole Championships
Willie Park Sr, 1860 and 1866; Tom Morris Sr, 1862 and 1864; Tommy Morris Jr, 1869 and 1870; Mungo Park, 1874; Jamie Anderson, 1879; Bob Ferguson, 1880, 1881, 1882; Willie Fernie, 1883; Jack Simpson, 1884; Hugh Kirkaldy, 1891

Largest Leads Since 1892

After 18 holes:
5 strokes: Sandy Herd, 1896
4 strokes: Harry Vardon, 1902; Jim Barnes, 1925; Christy O'Connor Jr, 1985
After 36 holes:
9 strokes: Henry Cotton, 1934
6 strokes: Abe Mitchell, 1920
After 54 holes:
10 strokes: Henry Cotton, 1934
7 strokes: Harry Vardon, 1903; Tony Lema, 1964
6 strokes: JH Taylor, 1900; James Braid, 1905; James Braid, 1908; Max Faulkner, 1951; Tom Lehman, 1996; Tiger Woods, 2000

Champions Who Had Four Rounds, Each Better than the One Before

Jack White, Royal St George's, 1904 – 80, 75, 72, 69
James Braid, Muirfield, 1906 – 77, 76, 74, 73
Ben Hogan, Carnoustie, 1953 – 73, 71, 70, 68
Gary Player, Muirfield, 1959 – 75, 71, 70, 68

Same Number of Strokes in Each of the Four Rounds by a Champion

Denny Shute, St Andrews, 1933 – 73, 73, 73, 73 (excluding the playoff)

Best 18-Hole Recovery by a Champion

George Duncan, Deal, 1920. Duncan was 13 strokes behind the leader, Abe Mitchell, after 36 holes and level with him after 54.

Greatest Variation Between Rounds by a Champion

14 strokes: Henry Cotton, 1934, second round 65, fourth round 79
12 strokes: Henry Cotton, 1934, first round 67, fourth round 79
11 strokes: Jack White, 1904, first round 80, fourth round 69; Greg Norman, 1986, first round 74, second round 63; Greg Norman, 1986, second round 63, third round 74
10 strokes: Seve Ballesteros, 1979, second round 65, third round 75

Greatest Variation Between Two Successive Rounds by a Champion

11 strokes: Greg Norman, 1986, first round 74, second round 63; Greg Norman, 1986, second round 63, third round 74
10 strokes: Seve Ballesteros, 1979, second round 65, third round 75

Greatest Comeback by a Champion

After 18 holes
Harry Vardon, 1896, 11 strokes behind the leader
After 36 holes
George Duncan, 1920, 13 strokes behind the leader
After 54 holes
Paul Lawrie, 1999, 10 strokes behind the leader

Champions Who Had Four Rounds Under 70

Greg Norman, Royal St George's, 1993 – 66, 68, 69, 64; Nick Price, Turnberry, 1994 – 69, 66, 67, 66; Tiger Woods, St Andrews, 2000 – 67, 66, 67, 69

Competitors Who Failed to Win The Open Despite Having Four Rounds Under 70

Ernie Els, Royal St George's, 1993 – 68, 69, 69, 68; Jesper Parnevik, Turnberry, 1994 – 68, 66, 68, 67; Ernie Els, Royal Troon, 2004 – 69, 69, 68, 68

Lowest Final Round by a Champion

64: Greg Norman, Royal St George's, 1993
65: Tom Watson, Turnberry, 1977; Seve Ballesteros, Royal Lytham & St Annes, 1988; Justin Leonard, Royal Troon, 1997

Worst Round by a Champion Since 1939

78: Fred Daly, third round, Royal Liverpool, 1947
76: Bobby Locke, second round, Royal St George's, 1949; Paul Lawrie, third round, Carnoustie, 1999

Champion with the Worst Finishing Round Since 1939

75: Sam Snead, St Andrews, 1946

Lowest Opening Round by a Champion

65: Louis Oosthuizen, St Andrews, 2010

Most Open Championship Appearances

46: Gary Player
38: Jack Nicklaus

Most Final Day Appearances Since 1892

32: Jack Nicklaus
31: Sandy Herd
30: JH Taylor
28: Ted Ray
27: Harry Vardon; James Braid; Nick Faldo
26: Peter Thomson; Gary Player

Stewart Cink (2009)

Most Appearances by a Champion Before His First Victory

19: Darren Clarke, 2011
15: Nick Price, 1994
14: Sandy Herd, 1902
13: Ted Ray, 1912; Jack White, 1904; Reg Whitcombe, 1938; Mark O'Meara, 1998
11: George Duncan, 1920; Nick Faldo, 1987; Ernie Els, 2002; Stewart Cink, 2009
10: Roberto de Vicenzo, 1967; Padraig Harrington, 2007

The Open Which Provided the Greatest Number of Rounds Under 70 Since 1946

148 rounds, Turnberry, 1994

The Open with the Fewest Rounds Under 70 Since 1946

2 rounds, St Andrews, 1946; Royal Liverpool, 1947; Carnoustie, 1968

Statistically Most Difficult Hole Since 1982

St Andrews, 1984, Par-4 17th, 4.79

Longest Course in Open History

Carnoustie, 2007, 7,421 yards

Number of Times Each Course Has Hosted The Open Championship

St Andrews, 28; Prestwick, 24; Muirfield, 15; Royal St George's, 14; Royal Liverpool, 11; Royal Lytham & St Annes, 10; Royal Birkdale, 9; Royal Troon, 8; Carnoustie, 7; Musselburgh, 6; Turnberry, 4; Royal Cinque Ports, 2; Royal Portrush and Prince's, 1

Prize Money

Year	Total	First Prize
1860	nil	nil
1863	10	nil
1864	15	6
1865	20	8
1866	11	6
1867	16	7
1868	12	6
1872	unknown	8
1873	unknown	11
1874	20	8
1876	27	10
1877	20	8
1878	unknown	8
1879	47	10
1880	unknown	8
1881	21	8
1882	47.25	12
1883	20	8
1884	23	8
1885	35.50	10
1886	20	8
1889	22	8
1890	29.50	13
1891	28.50	10
1892	110	35
1893	100	30
1900	125	50
1910	135	50
1920	225	75
1927	275	75
1930	400	100
1931	500	100
1946	1,000	150
1949	1,500	300
1951	1,700	300
1953	2,500	500
1954	3,500	750
1955	3,750	1,000
1958	4,850	1,000
1959	5,000	1,000
1960	7,000	1,250
1961	8,500	1,400
1963	8,500	1,500
1965	10,000	1,750
1966	15,000	2,100
1968	20,000	3,000
1969	30,000	4,250
1970	40,000	5,250
1971	45,000	5,500
1972	50,000	5,500
1975	75,000	7,500
1977	100,000	10,000
1978	125,000	12,500
1979	155,000	15,000

Year	Total	First Prize
1980	200,000	25,000
1982	250,000	32,000
1983	310,000	40,000
1984	451,000	55,000
1985	530,000	65,000
1986	600,000	70,000
1987	650,000	75,000
1988	700,000	80,000
1989	750,000	80,000
1990	825,000	85,000
1991	900,000	90,000
1992	950,000	95,000
1993	1,000,000	100,000
1994	1,100,000	110,000

Year	Total	First Prize
1995	1,250,000	125,000
1996	1,400,000	200,000
1997	1,600,000	250,000
1998	1,800,000	300,000
1999	2,000,000	350,000
2000	2,750,000	500,000
2001	3,300,000	600,000
2002	3,800,000	700,000
2003	3,900,000	700,000
2004	4,000,000	720,000
2007	4,200,000	750,000
2010	4,800,000	850,000
2011	5,000,000	900,000

Attendance

Year	Total	Year	Total	Year	Total
1960	39,563	1978	125,271	1996	170,000
1961	21,708	1979	134,501	1997	176,000
1962	37,098	1980	131,610	1998	195,100
1963	24,585	1981	111,987	1999	157,000
1964	35,954	1982	133,299	2000	230,000
1965	32,927	1983	142,892	2001	178,000
1966	40,182	1984	193,126	2002	161,500
1967	29,880	1985	141,619	2003	183,000
1968	51,819	1986	134,261	2004	176,000
1969	46,001	1987	139,189	2005	223,000
1970	81,593	1988	191,334	2006	230,000
1971	70,076	1989	160,639	2007	154,000
1972	84,746	1990	208,680	2008	201,500
1973	78,810	1991	189,435	2009	123,000
1974	92,796	1992	146,427	2010	201,000
1975	85,258	1993	141,000	2011	179,700
1976	92,021	1994	128,000		
1977	87,615	1995	180,000		

The 140th Open Championship

Complete Scores

HOLE			1	2	3	4	5	6	7	8	9	10	11	12	13	14	15	16	17	18	
PAR	POSITION		4	4	3	4	4	3	5	4	4	4	4	3	4	5	4	3	4	4	TOTAL
Darren Clarke	T6	Round 1	5	3	3	3	4	3	6	4	4	3	3	5	3	4	4	3	4	4	68
Northern Ireland	T1	Round 2	4	4	2	6	4	3	3	3	4	5	3	3	3	6	4	4	4	3	68
£90,000	1	Round 3	3	4	3	4	5	3	4	5	4	4	3	3	4	5	4	3	4	4	69
	1	Round 4	4	3	3	5	4	3	3	4	4	4	3	4	4	5	4	3	5	5	**70 -275**
Phil Mickelson	T36	Round 1	5	4	3	4	4	3	4	4	4	4	4	4	4	4	4	3	4	4	70
USA	T14	Round 2	4	4	4	4	4	3	4	4	4	4	3	4	4	4	4	3	4	4	69
£427,500	T7	Round 3	4	4	4	5	4	4	4	4	4	5	2	4	4	4	4	3	4	4	71
	T2	Round 4	4	3	3	3	4	2	3	4	4	3	4	4	5	5	5	4	4	4	**68 -278**
Dustin Johnson	T36	Round 1	4	5	3	4	4	3	5	4	5	5	3	5	4	4	3	1	3	5	70
USA	T7	Round 2	4	4	3	4	3	3	4	4	5	3	4	3	4	4	5	4	3	4	68
£427,500	2	Round 3	4	4	3	5	3	3	4	4	5	3	3	3	5	4	3	3	5	4	68
	T2	Round 4	4	4	4	4	4	4	4	4	3	3	3	4	7	4	3	4	4	5	**72 -278**
Thomas Bjorn	T1	Round 1	4	3	3	4	4	3	4	3	5	4	3	3	4	4	3	2	4	5	65
Denmark	T3	Round 2	4	5	4	5	3	3	4	4	4	3	3	5	4	6	4	3	4	4	72
£260,000	T3	Round 3	4	3	3	5	4	4	4	4	4	3	4	3	4	4	5	4	3	5	71
	4	Round 4	4	4	3	5	4	2	5	3	4	4	3	4	4	5	5	3	5	4	**71 -279**
Chad Campbell	T18	Round 1	4	4	3	5	4	2	5	4	3	4	2	4	5	4	5	3	4	4	69
USA	T3	Round 2	4	5	3	4	4	3	4	4	4	4	3	4	3	5	4	2	3	5	68
£181,667	T13	Round 3	4	4	4	5	4	2	5	4	4	5	3	4	4	5	5	3	4	5	74
	T5	Round 4	5	3	2	4	4	3	4	5	5	4	3	3	4	5	4	4	4	3	**69 -280**
Anthony Kim	T71	Round 1	4	4	3	6	4	2	4	5	4	4	3	4	5	5	4	3	4	4	72
USA	T19	Round 2	4	4	3	5	4	2	4	4	4	4	5	2	4	4	4	3	4	4	68
£181,667	T7	Round 3	5	4	3	5	5	3	5	5	3	4	3	3	4	4	3	3	4	4	70
	T5	Round 4	4	3	3	5	4	3	4	4	4	4	3	3	4	5	5	3	4	5	**70 -280**
Rickie Fowler	T36	Round 1	3	4	4	4	4	3	4	4	3	4	4	4	5	5	4	3	4	4	70
USA	T19	Round 2	4	3	4	4	4	4	4	4	5	4	3	4	4	5	3	3	4	4	70
£181,667	T3	Round 3	4	5	3	4	3	3	5	4	4	4	4	4	3	5	3	2	4	4	68
	T5	Round 4	4	4	3	4	4	3	5	4	4	4	4	4	6	4	4	4	4	4	**72 -280**
Raphael Jacquelin	T107	Round 1	4	5	4	4	4	3	5	4	4	4	3	4	5	5	4	4	4	4	74
France	T32	Round 2	5	4	3	3	3	3	4	4	4	4	4	4	3	4	4	4	3	4	67
£130,000	T17	Round 3	4	4	4	5	3	3	5	4	4	3	4	3	4	5	4	3	4	5	71
	8	Round 4	3	4	3	4	4	3	5	4	3	4	4	4	4	4	5	2	5	4	**69 -281**

* Denotes amateurs

HOLE			1	2	3	4	5	6	7	8	9	10	11	12	13	14	15	16	17	18	
PAR	POSITION		4	4	3	4	4	3	5	4	4	4	3	4	4	5	4	3	4	4	TOTAL
Sergio Garcia	T36	Round 1	4	4	3	5	4	3	5	4	3	4	3	3	3	5	4	4	4	5	70
Spain	T19	Round 2	4	4	3	4	4	3	5	4	4	4	3	4	3	4	5	3	5	4	70
£104,333	T25	Round 3	5	4	3	5	4	3	5	4	4	4	4	3	4	6	4	4	4	4	74
	T9	Round 4	4	3	3	3	3	3	4	6	4	4	3	4	5	5	4	2	5	3	68 **-282**
Simon Dyson	T6	Round 1	4	4	3	4	4	2	5	4	4	4	3	4	4	5	3	3	3	5	68
England	T19	Round 2	3	3	2	5	4	3	5	4	4	4	3	4	5	5	5	3	6	4	72
£104,333	T17	Round 3	4	4	3	5	4	4	4	4	5	5	2	4	4	4	4	3	4	5	72
	T9	Round 4	4	4	4	4	4	4	3	3	5	5	3	4	4	4	4	3	4	4	70 **-282**
Davis Love III	T36	Round 1	3	4	3	5	4	4	4	4	5	3	3	4	4	4	3	3	3	5	70
USA	T7	Round 2	4	4	2	4	4	2	5	4	4	4	3	4	5	4	4	4	4	3	68
£104,333	T7	Round 3	5	4	4	4	4	3	4	4	4	4	2	4	5	5	4	3	5	4	72
	T9	Round 4	5	3	4	4	4	3	4	5	4	4	3	4	4	5	5	3	4	4	72 **-282**
Steve Stricker	T18	Round 1	4	4	3	4	4	4	4	4	5	4	3	3	4	5	3	3	4	4	69
USA	T19	Round 2	4	3	3	5	4	3	6	3	4	3	4	3	4	5	4	4	5	4	71
£78,333	T17	Round 3	4	5	4	5	4	3	4	4	4	4	4	3	3	5	4	3	4	5	72
	T12	Round 4	5	5	3	5	4	3	4	4	4	4	5	3	4	4	4	2	4	4	71 **-283**
Martin Kaymer	T6	Round 1	4	4	3	4	4	4	4	4	4	4	2	4	4	5	4	2	4	4	68
Germany	T3	Round 2	4	4	3	4	4	3	4	5	4	4	3	4	4	4	4	3	4	4	69
£78,333	T7	Round 3	4	4	4	4	4	4	6	4	4	4	4	3	4	5	3	4	4	4	73
	T12	Round 4	4	4	3	5	4	3	6	5	5	3	3	3	5	5	4	2	5	4	73 **-283**
Lucas Glover	T3	Round 1	4	5	3	4	4	3	5	4	3	3	3	4	4	5	4	2	3	3	66
USA	T1	Round 2	4	3	3	5	4	3	4	4	4	5	3	4	4	5	4	3	4	4	70
£78,333	T5	Round 3	5	4	3	4	4	3	5	4	4	4	3	5	4	5	4	3	5	4	73
	T12	Round 4	4	4	4	5	4	4	5	4	5	4	3	4	4	5	4	2	4	5	74 **-283**
George Coetzee	T18	Round 1	4	4	3	4	5	3	4	4	5	5	3	3	5	4	3	3	4	4	69
South Africa	T7	Round 2	5	3	3	5	4	4	4	3	3	4	4	3	4	4	5	3	4	4	69
£68,000	T7	Round 3	4	4	3	5	4	4	4	4	3	4	4	4	4	4	6	3	4	4	72
	15	Round 4	5	4	3	5	4	4	4	4	4	6	3	3	4	5	4	5	3	4	74 **-284**
Richard Green	T36	Round 1	4	4	3	3	4	3	6	4	4	5	3	3	4	4	4	3	5	4	70
Australia	T32	Round 2	4	4	2	5	4	3	6	4	4	4	4	3	4	5	5	3	4	3	71
£56,000	T25	Round 3	4	5	4	4	4	4	4	5	4	4	4	4	4	4	4	3	4	4	73
	T16	Round 4	5	3	3	5	4	3	3	4	5	5	3	4	4	4	4	3	4	5	71 **-285**
Charl Schwartzel	T51	Round 1	4	4	2	5	4	4	4	4	5	3	4	5	5	4	4	3	3	4	71
South Africa	T7	Round 2	4	3	2	4	3	3	5	4	5	3	2	4	4	5	5	3	4	4	67
£56,000	T22	Round 3	4	4	4	6	4	3	4	5	4	4	3	4	4	6	4	3	4	5	75
	T16	Round 4	3	4	4	4	4	4	4	4	3	5	3	4	3	7	5	3	4	4	72 **-285**
YE Yang	T51	Round 1	4	4	4	5	4	3	5	4	4	4	3	4	4	4	4	3	4	4	71
Korea	T19	Round 2	4	4	3	4	4	3	5	5	4	4	3	3	3	4	4	3	4	5	69
£56,000	T22	Round 3	5	3	3	5	4	3	4	4	5	4	4	4	4	5	4	3	4	5	73
	T16	Round 4	4	4	3	5	3	3	6	4	4	4	3	4	4	6	5	2	4	4	72 **-285**
Fredrik Jacobson	T36	Round 1	3	4	3	4	4	4	5	5	3	3	3	5	4	4	4	3	4	5	70
Sweden	T19	Round 2	3	5	3	5	4	3	3	5	4	5	2	3	4	4	4	3	5	5	70
£56,000	T22	Round 3	4	4	4	5	4	4	5	4	5	4	3	4	3	5	4	2	4	5	73
	T16	Round 4	4	4	3	4	4	2	4	4	5	5	3	4	4	5	5	3	4	5	72 **-285**
Webb Simpson	T3	Round 1	4	4	3	4	4	3	5	4	4	3	3	3	4	5	4	3	3	3	66
USA	T19	Round 2	4	4	3	6	4	3	5	4	5	4	3	4	4	5	5	3	4	4	74
£56,000	T17	Round 3	5	4	4	4	3	3	4	4	4	4	3	4	4	7	4	3	4	4	72
	T16	Round 4	4	4	3	5	3	4	4	6	4	4	3	4	4	5	5	3	4	4	73 **-285**

HOLE		1	2	3	4	5	6	7	8	9	10	11	12	13	14	15	16	17	18	
PAR	POSITION	4	4	3	4	4	3	5	4	4	4	3	4	4	5	4	3	4	4	TOTAL
Zach Johnson	T71	Round 1	5	4	3	4	6	4	5	4	4	4	2	4	4	4	4	3	3	5	72
USA	T19	Round 2	4	4	2	5	4	3	5	4	4	4	2	4	4	5	4	2	4	4	68
£56,000	T13	Round 3	4	4	3	6	4	2	5	5	4	4	3	4	4	4	4	3	4	5	71
	T16	Round 4	4	4	3	4	4	4	4	4	5	5	4	4	4	4	4	4	4	5	74 **-285**
Tom Watson	T71	Round 1	4	4	2	4	5	3	5	4	4	4	4	3	4	6	5	3	4	4	72
USA	T45	Round 2	4	4	3	4	4	1	4	4	5	5	4	3	4	6	4	3	3	5	70
£44,667	T25	Round 3	4	4	3	4	4	3	4	4	4	4	4	5	4	5	5	2	4	5	72
	T22	Round 4	4	4	3	4	5	4	4	5	4	4	3	4	5	4	4	3	4	4	72 **-286**
Tom Lehman	T51	Round 1	5	4	3	4	4	4	6	4	4	3	2	3	4	5	4	3	4	5	71
USA	T7	Round 2	4	3	3	4	4	3	4	5	4	4	3	3	4	4	4	3	4	4	67
£44,667	T13	Round 3	4	4	4	5	4	4	4	4	3	4	3	4	5	5	4	4	3	5	73
	T22	Round 4	4	4	3	5	4	4	5	4	4	5	3	3	5	6	4	4	4	4	75 **-286**
Anders Hansen	T18	Round 1	4	3	3	5	4	3	5	4	5	3	3	4	3	4	4	3	4	5	69
Denmark	T7	Round 2	4	3	3	4	5	3	4	4	4	4	4	3	4	4	4	3	5	4	69
£44,667	T7	Round 3	4	4	3	5	4	4	4	5	2	4	3	4	4	5	4	3	4	6	72
	T22	Round 4	4	4	4	6	5	3	5	5	4	4	3	4	4	5	4	3	5	4	76 **-286**
Rory McIlroy	T51	Round 1	5	4	4	4	4	3	5	3	4	4	3	4	5	5	4	3	3	4	71
Northern Ireland	T19	Round 2	4	4	3	4	4	2	4	5	4	5	3	4	3	4	5	3	4	4	69
£39,000	T25	Round 3	5	4	4	4	4	3	4	5	4	4	3	4	4	7	4	3	4	4	74
	T25	Round 4	4	3	5	4	4	3	6	4	4	4	3	4	3	5	4	3	5	5	73 **-287**
Adam Scott	T18	Round 1	4	4	2	4	4	3	5	4	3	4	4	4	4	5	5	3	4	3	69
Australia	T14	Round 2	4	4	3	4	4	2	6	4	4	4	4	4	4	5	4	3	4	3	70
£39,000	T17	Round 3	4	5	3	6	4	3	5	5	4	3	3	4	4	4	4	4	4	4	73
	T25	Round 4	4	4	3	4	4	3	5	5	4	6	4	4	5	5	4	3	4	4	75 **-287**
Miguel Angel Jimenez	T3	Round 1	4	4	2	3	4	3	5	4	3	4	3	3	4	5	4	3	3	4	66
Spain	T3	Round 2	4	5	3	5	4	2	4	4	5	3	3	3	4	5	5	3	4	4	71
	T5	Round 3	4	4	3	5	4	4	5	4	4	3	4	4	4	5	4	3	4	4	72
£39,000	**T25**	Round 4	5	3	4	7	4	4	5	4	4	4	4	4	4	5	4	3	5	5	78 **-287**
Ryan Moore	T18	Round 1	4	4	2	4	4	3	4	5	4	4	3	4	4	4	4	3	5	4	69
USA	T59	Round 2	4	5	3	4	4	3	4	5	4	5	5	4	4	5	4	3	4	4	74
£35,250	T55	Round 3	4	5	3	6	3	3	4	6	4	4	3	4	5	5	4	3	5	5	76
	T28	Round 4	5	3	3	4	4	2	5	4	3	4	3	5	4	5	4	4	4	3	69 **-288**
Charles Howell III	T51	Round 1	4	4	3	4	4	3	5	5	4	4	4	4	4	5	4	3	4	3	71
USA	T32	Round 2	3	4	3	4	3	3	4	5	4	5	3	3	4	5	5	2	5	5	70
£35,250	T25	Round 3	4	4	3	5	4	4	5	4	4	4	3	4	4	5	5	3	4	4	73
	T28	Round 4	4	4	4	4	4	2	5	5	5	4	4	4	4	5	5	3	4	4	74 **-288**
Stewart Cink	T36	Round 1	4	4	3	4	5	2	5	3	4	3	2	4	5	5	5	3	4	5	70
USA	T32	Round 2	3	4	4	4	3	4	4	6	3	4	3	4	4	5	5	3	4	4	71
£29,214	T48	Round 3	5	5	4	4	4	4	5	4	5	5	4	4	4	4	5	3	4	4	77
	T30	Round 4	4	4	2	4	4	3	5	4	4	4	3	4	4	5	5	4	4	4	71 **-289**
Jason Day	T51	Round 1	5	4	2	4	5	4	4	4	4	4	4	3	5	3	5	3	4	4	71
Australia	T32	Round 2	3	4	3	6	4	3	3	5	3	4	3	4	4	5	4	3	5	4	70
£29,214	T41	Round 3	4	4	3	6	5	3	6	5	4	3	3	4	4	5	4	4	5	4	76
	T30	Round 4	4	4	3	5	4	3	4	4	4	4	3	4	5	5	4	3	5	4	72 **-289**
Gary Woodland	T126	Round 1	5	4	5	4	4	4	4	4	6	5	3	3	5	5	4	2	4	4	75
USA	T59	Round 2	5	4	3	5	4	3	4	3	4	3	3	4	4	5	3	3	4	4	68
£29,214	T41	Round 3	4	4	3	4	3	3	4	4	4	4	3	5	5	8	3	4	5	4	74
	T30	Round 4	4	3	3	5	3	3	4	4	4	5	3	5	5	5	5	2	5	4	72 **-289**

HOLE			1	2	3	4	5	6	7	8	9	10	11	12	13	14	15	16	17	18	
PAR	POSITION		4	4	3	4	4	3	5	4	4	4	3	4	4	5	4	3	4	4	TOTAL
Seung-Yul Noh	T18	Round 1	4	4	4	4	4	3	5	4	4	4	3	4	4	5	4	2	3	4	69
Korea	T32	Round 2	5	4	3	5	3	3	5	5	4	3	4	4	3	5	4	3	5	4	72
£29,214	T37	Round 3	4	5	3	5	4	3	5	6	5	4	4	4	3	5	4	3	4	4	75
	T30	Round 4	4	4	3	4	4	3	4	5	4	4	2	4	4	5	4	4	6	5	73 -289
Tom Lewis*	T1	Round 1	4	4	2	4	4	3	4	3	4	4	4	4	5	4	3	2	3	4	65
England	T14	Round 2	4	4	3	5	4	4	5	4	4	4	3	5	3	5	4	3	5	5	74
	T33	Round 3	4	4	4	5	5	3	5	5	5	4	3	4	4	5	5	3	3	5	76
	T30	Round 4	5	3	3	4	4	3	3	4	6	3	3	5	4	8	4	3	5	4	74 -289
Bubba Watson	T18	Round 1	4	4	3	4	3	3	5	4	4	4	3	4	4	5	4	3	4	4	69
USA	T32	Round 2	4	4	3	5	3	3	4	4	3	4	3	5	4	5	5	3	4	6	72
£29,214	T33	Round 3	4	4	4	5	4	3	5	5	4	4	3	3	5	5	4	3	4	5	74
	T30	Round 4	4	4	3	4	5	3	4	5	4	4	4	5	4	5	4	4	4	4	74 -289
Pablo Larrazabal	T6	Round 1	4	4	3	4	4	3	5	4	4	3	4	3	4	4	4	3	4	4	68
Spain	T7	Round 2	4	4	3	4	4	3	5	3	5	3	3	4	4	6	4	3	4	4	70
£29,214	T25	Round 3	5	4	4	5	4	3	5	4	5	4	3	5	4	5	4	3	5	4	76
	T30	Round 4	4	4	4	6	5	3	5	3	5	4	3	4	4	5	3	4	5	4	75 -289
Ryan Palmer	T6	Round 1	4	4	2	5	4	2	4	5	4	4	3	3	4	4	4	4	4	4	68
USA	T14	Round 2	4	4	4	4	4	3	4	5	4	5	3	5	3	4	4	2	4	5	71
£29,214	T13	Round 3	5	4	3	5	4	3	5	5	5	4	3	4	3	4	4	3	4	4	72
	T30	Round 4	4	3	4	6	5	3	5	4	5	6	3	4	4	5	4	3	5	5	78 -289
Simon Khan	T51	Round 1	4	4	3	4	4	3	5	4	4	4	3	4	4	5	5	3	4	4	71
England	T59	Round 2	3	4	5	4	4	4	4	4	5	4	3	3	4	5	5	3	4	4	72
£22,500	T59	Round 3	4	4	4	5	4	4	4	6	4	4	4	4	3	6	5	3	5	4	77
	T38	Round 4	4	4	2	4	3	3	4	4	4	4	4	4	5	5	5	3	4	4	70 -290
Jeff Overton	T6	Round 1	4	4	3	5	4	3	5	4	3	4	3	4	3	4	4	3	4	4	68
USA	T14	Round 2	3	4	4	4	4	3	4	4	5	3	3	4	5	5	4	4	4	4	71
£22,500	T41	Round 3	4	5	3	5	5	3	5	4	4	4	3	4	4	6	6	3	5	5	78
	T38	Round 4	4	3	4	4	4	4	5	4	4	4	2	4	4	5	5	4	5	4	73 -290
Gary Boyd	T51	Round 1	3	4	3	5	5	3	4	4	4	4	3	4	4	4	5	3	4	5	71
England	T32	Round 2	5	3	3	4	4	4	4	4	4	4	4	4	4	4	5	3	4	3	70
£22,500	T41	Round 3	4	4	4	5	4	3	5	5	4	5	4	4	4	5	4	4	4	4	76
	T38	Round 4	5	5	3	4	3	4	5	4	4	4	3	3	4	5	4	4	4	5	73 -290
Yuta Ikeda	T18	Round 1	4	4	3	4	4	3	5	4	4	3	3	4	4	4	4	3	5	4	69
Japan	T19	Round 2	4	3	3	7	4	2	5	4	3	4	3	3	4	4	5	4	5	4	71
£22,500	T33	Round 3	4	4	4	5	4	4	5	5	3	4	3	5	4	5	4	3	5	4	75
	T38	Round 4	4	3	3	5	4	3	4	6	5	6	4	3	4	5	4	3	5	4	75 -290
Robert Rock	T18	Round 1	4	3	4	4	4	3	5	4	4	4	4	3	4	5	4	3	3	4	69
England	T19	Round 2	4	4	3	5	4	3	5	4	4	5	3	4	4	4	4	2	4	5	71
£22,500	T25	Round 3	4	4	3	5	4	3	5	5	4	5	4	4	4	4	5	3	4	4	74
	T38	Round 4	4	4	4	5	4	4	5	5	4	4	2	4	4	6	4	3	5	5	76 -290
Trevor Immelman	T36	Round 1	4	4	3	3	5	5	5	5	4	4	3	3	4	5	4	3	3	3	70
South Africa	T45	Round 2	4	3	3	5	4	3	5	4	4	5	3	4	5	5	4	3	4	4	72
£22,500	T25	Round 3	5	5	3	4	4	3	4	4	3	4	4	4	5	5	4	3	4	4	72
	T38	Round 4	4	4	3	5	4	3	5	4	4	4	3	4	4	5	5	4	6	5	76 -290
Spencer Levin	T71	Round 1	4	4	2	4	5	3	6	5	4	4	3	3	4	5	4	3	4	5	72
USA	T32	Round 2	4	4	3	5	3	3	4	5	3	4	3	4	4	3	4	3	5	5	69
£17,688	68	Round 3	4	4	4	8	4	4	4	5	5	6	4	5	4	6	5	2	4	4	81
	T44	Round 4	3	3	3	4	4	3	4	5	4	3	4	4	4	5	4	4	4	4	69 -291

HOLE			1	2	3	4	5	6	7	8	9	10	11	12	13	14	15	16	17	18	
PAR	POSITION		4	4	3	4	4	3	5	4	4	4	3	4	4	5	4	3	4	4	TOTAL
Justin Rose	T71	Round 1	4	4	3	4	4	3	5	4	4	4	4	4	4	6	4	3	4	4	72
England	T45	Round 2	4	3	3	4	4	3	4	4	4	4	4	4	4	4	4	3	5	5	70
£17,688	T63	Round 3	5	5	4	5	4	3	5	4	4	5	4	4	4	6	5	3	4	5	79
	T44	Round 4	4	4	3	5	3	4	3	3	5	4	2	4	5	4	4	4	4	5	70 -**291**
KJ Choi	T51	Round 1	4	4	4	4	4	3	5	4	3	5	3	4	4	5	6	2	4	3	71
Korea	T59	Round 2	4	4	3	4	5	3	6	4	5	3	4	4	4	5	4	2	4	4	72
£17,688	T48	Round 3	4	3	3	6	5	4	4	5	5	4	3	4	4	5	5	3	4	4	75
	T44	Round 4	4	3	4	5	4	3	6	4	3	5	3	4	4	5	4	3	5	4	73 -**291**
Kyle Stanley	T6	Round 1	5	4	3	4	4	3	5	3	4	4	2	3	4	5	4	2	4	5	68
USA	T19	Round 2	4	4	3	4	4	3	3	5	4	5	3	4	4	5	4	3	6	4	72
£17,688	T41	Round 3	4	4	4	5	4	4	5	5	4	4	4	5	3	5	5	3	4	5	77
	T44	Round 4	4	4	4	4	3	3	4	4	4	5	4	5	4	4	6	3	5	4	74 -**291**
Gregory Bourdy	T91	Round 1	4	4	3	4	5	3	5	4	4	4	3	4	3	5	4	3	5	6	73
France	T59	Round 2	4	4	2	4	5	3	4	5	4	4	2	4	5	5	4	3	4	4	70
£14,600	T59	Round 3	4	4	3	6	4	3	5	5	4	4	2	5	4	6	5	4	4	5	77
	T48	Round 4	4	4	3	4	4	3	5	4	4	4	4	4	5	5	4	3	4	4	72 -**292**
Floris De Vries	T36	Round 1	4	3	3	5	4	3	5	4	5	4	4	3	4	5	4	3	4	3	70
Netherlands	T59	Round 2	4	5	3	5	5	3	3	4	4	6	2	5	4	5	4	3	4	4	73
£14,600	T55	Round 3	4	3	4	4	4	4	5	5	4	5	3	4	3	6	5	3	5	5	76
	T48	Round 4	4	4	4	5	4	3	3	5	4	5	5	4	3	6	4	3	4	3	73 -**292**
Jim Furyk	T71	Round 1	4	4	3	4	5	4	4	5	5	4	3	4	4	4	5	3	3	4	72
USA	T45	Round 2	5	3	2	4	3	4	5	4	4	4	3	4	5	5	4	3	4	4	70
£14,600	T48	Round 3	4	5	3	5	4	4	4	5	4	5	3	5	4	5	4	3	4	5	76
	T48	Round 4	4	4	3	5	4	3	6	5	5	4	2	4	3	5	4	3	5	5	74 -**292**
Peter Uihlein*	T51	Round 1	5	4	4	4	4	4	5	4	4	3	4	4	4	4	4	3	4	3	71
USA	T45	Round 2	5	4	2	4	3	2	4	5	6	4	3	4	4	5	5	3	4	4	71
	T41	Round 3	4	5	3	5	4	4	5	4	3	3	3	4	5	6	4	3	4	6	75
	T48	Round 4	4	4	3	5	4	3	4	4	4	5	3	4	5	5	6	3	5	4	75 -**292**
Robert Allenby	T18	Round 1	4	3	3	5	4	2	5	5	5	4	3	4	4	5	4	2	3	4	69
Australia	T32	Round 2	4	4	3	4	4	3	4	4	4	5	2	4	4	5	6	3	5	4	72
£14,600	T37	Round 3	4	5	3	5	5	4	4	5	3	4	4	4	4	5	5	3	4	4	75
	T48	Round 4	5	3	4	4	5	3	4	4	5	6	3	4	4	6	4	3	4	5	76 -**292**
Richard McEvoy	T18	Round 1	5	4	3	4	4	3	4	4	5	3	3	4	4	5	4	3	3	4	69
England	T32	Round 2	4	4	3	5	4	4	5	5	4	4	3	5	4	5	4	2	3	4	72
£14,600	T37	Round 3	5	5	3	4	5	3	4	6	4	5	3	4	4	5	4	3	4	4	75
	T48	Round 4	5	4	4	5	3	3	4	4	4	5	3	4	4	6	5	4	4	5	76 -**292**
Paul Casey	T107	Round 1	4	4	4	4	5	3	6	4	4	5	3	4	4	6	3	3	4	4	74
England	T59	Round 2	3	4	3	5	3	3	4	4	4	4	4	4	4	4	5	3	4	4	69
£13,300	T63	Round 3	4	4	3	5	5	4	5	4	5	4	3	4	4	7	5	3	4	5	78
	T54	Round 4	4	4	3	5	5	3	4	4	3	4	2	5	4	5	4	4	5	4	72 -**293**
Rory Sabbatini	T51	Round 1	4	4	4	4	4	4	5	4	4	4	3	4	4	5	5	2	4	3	71
South Africa	T32	Round 2	4	4	3	5	4	3	4	4	3	4	2	4	4	5	4	3	5	5	70
£13,300	T48	Round 3	4	4	3	5	4	3	4	4	5	5	3	5	5	5	5	4	5	4	77
	T54	Round 4	4	5	3	5	3	3	4	6	4	4	3	4	3	6	4	4	5	5	75 -**293**
Louis Oosthuizen	T71	Round 1	4	4	4	4	4	4	5	5	4	5	2	4	4	5	4	3	3	4	72
South Africa	T45	Round 2	4	4	3	4	4	3	5	5	5	3	3	4	4	4	4	2	4	5	70
£13,300	T37	Round 3	4	4	3	5	4	4	4	4	5	5	3	4	4	5	5	2	5	4	74
	T54	Round 4	4	4	4	5	4	4	5	5	4	5	3	4	5	5	5	3	4	4	77 -**293**

		HOLE	1	2	3	4	5	6	7	8	9	10	11	12	13	14	15	16	17	18	
	POSITION	PAR	4	4	3	4	4	3	5	4	4	4	3	4	4	5	4	3	4	4	TOTAL
Bill Haas	T71	Round 1	4	4	3	5	5	2	6	5	4	4	3	3	4	4	4	3	4	5	72
USA	T45	Round 2	4	4	3	5	4	3	5	4	4	5	3	3	4	5	4	3	4	3	70
£12,750	T63	Round 3	4	4	4	4	4	3	4	5	4	5	3	4	4	5	6	4	6	6	79
	T57	Round 4	4	3	3	5	4	2	4	7	4	4	3	4	4	6	4	4	4	4	73 **-294**
Gregory Havret	T71	Round 1	3	5	2	4	5	3	5	4	5	4	4	5	4	4	4	3	4	4	72
France	T59	Round 2	3	5	3	6	3	3	5	4	4	4	3	4	4	4	4	3	5	4	71
£12,750	T63	Round 3	5	4	3	5	3	3	4	4	5	4	2	5	5	10	4	3	4	5	78
	T57	Round 4	4	4	3	5	4	3	5	3	4	4	4	4	4	5	4	4	4	5	73 **-294**
Ricky Barnes	T6	Round 1	4	4	3	3	5	3	4	4	3	4	3	4	4	5	4	3	4	4	68
USA	T45	Round 2	4	4	3	3	4	3	4	4	4	5	4	4	3	8	5	3	4	5	74
£12,750	T59	Round 3	5	4	3	5	4	4	4	4	4	5	4	5	5	5	5	3	4	5	78
	T57	Round 4	4	4	4	4	5	3	4	3	3	4	3	4	5	8	5	3	4	4	74 **-294**
Fredrik Andersson Hed	T6	Round 1	4	3	3	4	3	3	5	4	3	4	3	5	4	6	3	3	4	4	68
	T59	Round 2	4	5	3	4	3	3	6	4	4	5	4	3	5	5	4	4	5	4	75
Sweden	T59	Round 3	5	4	4	4	4	4	5	4	5	4	4	4	4	5	6	3	4	4	77
£12,750	**T57**	Round 4	4	4	3	5	4	3	5	5	5	5	5	3	5	4	5	4	3	3	74 **-294**
Stephen Gallacher	T36	Round 1	4	4	3	5	4	3	5	5	5	3	3	4	4	4	4	3	3	4	70
Scotland	T32	Round 2	4	3	3	4	3	3	4	4	4	5	4	3	4	6	5	3	4	5	71
£12,750	T48	Round 3	4	5	4	5	4	3	4	5	6	5	3	4	5	5	3	3	4	5	77
	T57	Round 4	4	4	4	5	4	3	4	4	4	5	4	4	5	6	4	4	4	4	76 **-294**
Bo Van Pelt	T91	Round 1	4	4	3	4	5	3	5	4	5	5	3	4	4	4	3	4	4	5	73
USA	T45	Round 2	5	4	4	4	4	3	4	4	4	3	4	4	3	4	4	4	4	4	69
£12,750	T33	Round 3	4	4	3	5	4	3	5	4	4	5	3	4	4	5	4	3	4	5	73
	T57	Round 4	5	4	4	5	4	2	4	4	5	6	3	5	5	6	5	3	4	5	79 **-294**
Matthew Millar	T51	Round 1	4	5	3	4	4	3	5	5	3	4	2	4	5	5	4	3	4	4	71
Australia	T59	Round 2	4	5	3	6	4	2	4	4	4	4	4	5	4	4	4	3	4	4	72
£12,300	69	Round 3	4	4	3	6	4	4	5	5	4	5	3	3	5	6	4	4	5	6	80
	T63	Round 4	4	4	3	4	4	3	6	3	4	5	3	5	4	5	5	2	5	4	73 **-296**
Joost Luiten	T91	Round 1	5	4	4	4	4	4	5	3	5	4	3	4	4	4	5	3	4	4	73
Netherlands	T45	Round 2	4	4	3	4	4	3	4	3	4	3	3	4	4	6	4	3	4	4	69
£12,300	T63	Round 3	4	5	4	5	3	3	5	6	4	5	4	5	4	5	3	5	5	79
	T63	Round 4	4	4	3	4	4	3	4	6	6	4	4	4	4	4	4	2	6	5	75 **-296**
Mark Wilson	T107	Round 1	4	3	3	7	4	6	5	3	5	3	4	4	4	4	4	3	4	4	74
USA	T45	Round 2	4	4	3	4	4	3	4	3	4	4	3	4	3	4	5	3	5	4	68
£12,300	T41	Round 3	5	5	3	5	4	2	4	5	4	4	3	4	4	5	5	3	5	5	75
	T63	Round 4	5	4	3	4	4	4	4	5	5	5	4	5	4	4	4	4	6	5	79 **-296**
Paul Lawrie	T91	Round 1	4	5	3	4	4	3	5	4	4	4	4	4	4	5	5	3	3	5	73
Scotland	T59	Round 2	4	5	3	4	4	3	4	4	4	4	3	4	3	5	5	3	4	4	70
£12,050	T70	Round 3	4	4	4	7	5	3	3	5	5	4	3	5	3	7	5	4	5	5	81
	T66	Round 4	4	3	4	4	4	3	4	5	4	5	3	4	4	6	5	3	4	4	73 **-297**
Edoardo Molinari	T18	Round 1	4	4	3	4	4	2	6	3	5	3	3	5	5	5	4	2	4	3	69
Italy	T59	Round 2	5	3	3	4	4	3	4	4	4	5	3	4	4	8	5	3	4	4	74
£12,050	T55	Round 3	4	4	3	4	5	3	5	5	5	5	3	4	5	4	4	3	5	5	76
	T66	Round 4	4	4	3	4	4	4	5	5	5	5	3	5	6	4	4	3	5	5	78 **-297**
Henrik Stenson	T71	Round 1	4	4	4	4	4	3	5	4	4	4	3	4	4	5	5	2	4	5	72
Sweden	T59	Round 2	4	4	4	5	4	3	3	4	4	5	3	4	3	7	3	2	4	5	71
£11,900	T48	Round 3	4	4	4	4	4	3	4	4	4	5	4	5	5	5	4	4	4	4	75
	68	Round 4	4	4	4	4	4	3	5	4	4	4	4	4	5	11	4	3	4	5	80 **-298**

HOLE			1	2	3	4	5	6	7	8	9	10	11	12	13	14	15	16	17	18	
PAR	POSITION		4	4	3	4	4	3	5	4	4	4	3	4	4	5	4	3	4	4	TOTAL
Harrison Frazar	T71	Round 1	4	4	3	5	5	4	4	4	4	4	4	4	3	6	4	3	3	4	72
USA	T45	Round 2	4	4	3	4	4	3	5	4	4	4	3	4	4	7	3	3	3	4	70
£11,800	T55	Round 3	4	4	4	5	4	5	5	4	3	5	3	4	5	5	5	4	4	4	77
	69	Round 4	4	4	5	4	4	5	3	6	4	6	2	5	4	6	4	5	5	4	**80 -299**
Kenneth Ferrie	T51	Round 1	4	5	3	4	5	3	4	5	4	4	3	4	5	4	4	2	3	5	71
England	T45	Round 2	4	4	3	5	5	3	4	4	4	4	3	4	4	4	5	3	4	4	71
£11,700	T48	Round 3	4	4	4	5	4	3	4	5	6	4	4	4	4	5	4	3	5	4	76
	70	Round 4	4	5	4	4	4	3	5	4	7	4	4	4	5	5	7	3	6	5	**83 -301**
Jung-Gon Hwang	T6	Round 1	5	4	3	4	3	3	4	4	4	4	3	3	4	5	4	3	3	5	68
Korea	T45	Round 2	4	4	3	5	3	3	4	4	5	3	3	6	4	5	4	4	5	5	74
£11,600	71	Round 3	5	5	4	5	5	3	4	5	4	5	3	3	6	8	5	4	5	4	83
	71	Round 4	4	4	3	6	6	5	4	3	4	4	3	4	5	5	5	3	5	6	**79 -304**

NON QUALIFIERS AFTER 36 HOLES

(Leading 10 professionals and ties receive £3,500 each, next 20 professionals and ties receive £2,850 each, next 20 professionals and ties receive £2,600 each, remainder of professionals receive £2,350 each.)

HOLE			1	2	3	4	5	6	7	8	9	10	11	12	13	14	15	16	17	18	
PAR	POSITION		4	4	3	4	4	3	5	4	4	4	3	4	4	5	4	3	4	4	TOTAL
Thomas Aiken	T107	Round 1	5	4	4	5	5	2	5	4	4	3	3	5	4	6	4	3	4	4	74
South Africa	**T72**	Round 2	4	3	3	4	4	3	5	3	5	3	4	4	4	5	5	3	4	4	**70 -144**
Bryden Macpherson*	T51	Round 1	4	5	3	3	5	3	5	3	4	5	3	4	4	5	4	3	3	5	71
Australia	**T72**	Round 2	4	4	3	4	4	3	6	5	4	4	3	4	3	5	4	3	5	5	**73 -144**
Padraig Harrington	T91	Round 1	5	5	2	4	5	3	4	5	4	4	4	4	5	6	3	3	3	4	73
Republic of Ireland	**T72**	Round 2	5	4	3	3	5	2	5	4	4	5	3	3	4	6	4	3	4	4	**71 -144**
Lee Westwood	T51	Round 1	4	4	4	5	5	3	4	4	5	3	4	4	4	4	3	3	4	4	71
England	**T72**	Round 2	3	5	3	4	4	4	4	4	6	5	4	3	4	4	5	3	4	4	**73 -144**
JB Holmes	T18	Round 1	4	4	4	4	3	4	3	4	4	3	4	4	4	5	5	3	3	4	69
USA	**T72**	Round 2	5	4	4	5	3	2	4	5	4	5	4	4	4	7	4	2	5	4	**75 -144**
Alejandro Canizares	T91	Round 1	4	4	3	4	5	2	5	4	4	3	4	4	3	8	5	3	4	4	73
Spain	**T72**	Round 2	4	4	4	4	4	3	5	4	4	4	3	5	4	5	3	2	4	5	**71 -144**
Justin Leonard	T36	Round 1	3	3	2	5	4	3	5	4	4	4	3	4	4	5	5	3	4	5	70
USA	**T72**	Round 2	4	4	4	4	4	4	4	4	4	4	3	5	4	6	5	3	4	4	**74 -144**
Ben Crane	T51	Round 1	4	5	3	5	4	3	5	3	4	3	3	5	4	4	4	3	5	4	71
USA	**T72**	Round 2	4	5	3	5	3	3	4	5	5	5	3	4	3	4	4	4	4	5	**73 -144**
Danny Willett	T18	Round 1	4	4	3	4	4	3	4	4	5	3	3	4	5	5	3	3	4	4	69
England	**T72**	Round 2	4	5	3	6	4	4	4	4	5	4	4	5	3	4	4	3	5	4	**75 -144**
Graeme Storm	T36	Round 1	4	4	2	5	3	4	5	4	4	3	3	3	4	5	5	3	4	5	70
England	**T72**	Round 2	5	4	3	4	4	4	3	4	4	3	4	4	5	5	4	4	4	6	**74 -144**
Hunter Mahan	T126	Round 1	5	4	3	5	4	3	6	6	4	3	4	4	6	4	4	3	4	3	75
USA	**T72**	Round 2	4	3	3	5	4	4	4	4	4	4	2	4	4	4	4	3	4	5	**69 -144**
Ross Fisher	T51	Round 1	4	4	3	4	4	3	5	5	4	4	3	4	4	5	4	3	4	4	71
England	**T72**	Round 2	4	5	3	5	4	3	5	4	5	4	3	3	4	5	4	3	5	4	**73 -144**
Peter Hanson	T91	Round 1	4	4	4	4	3	2	5	5	5	4	3	4	5	5	4	3	4	5	73
Sweden	**T72**	Round 2	5	4	3	4	4	3	5	5	4	4	3	3	4	5	4	3	4	4	**71 -144**

			HOLE	1	2	3	4	5	6	7	8	9	10	11	12	13	14	15	16	17	18	
	POSITION		PAR	4	4	3	4	4	3	5	4	4	4	3	4	4	5	4	3	4	4	TOTAL
Sean O'Hair	T91	Round 1		4	5	4	4	4	3	5	4	4	4	4	4	3	6	5	2	4	4	73
USA	T72	Round 2		5	4	4	3	4	3	4	4	5	5	3	4	3	4	3	3	4	6	71 -144
Rick Kulacz	T107	Round 1		5	4	3	4	5	3	4	5	4	4	3	4	4	5	5	3	4	5	74
Australia	T72	Round 2		4	5	2	4	4	3	4	5	4	5	3	3	4	5	3	3	4	5	70 -144
Peter Whiteford	T36	Round 1		4	4	3	3	4	3	5	3	5	4	3	4	4	5	4	3	4	5	70
Scotland	T87	Round 2		4	4	3	5	3	4	5	4	4	4	3	4	6	5	4	4	5	4	75 -145
Brandt Snedeker	T126	Round 1		4	6	3	4	4	3	6	5	4	4	4	4	4	5	4	3	4	4	75
USA	T87	Round 2		5	4	2	4	4	3	4	4	4	4	3	4	4	4	4	3	5	5	70 -145
Graeme McDowell	T6	Round 1		6	4	3	4	5	2	4	5	4	4	3	3	3	5	4	3	3	3	68
Northern Ireland	T87	Round 2		4	4	4	4	4	4	5	5	6	4	4	4	5	5	4	3	4	4	77 -145
Nick Watney	T107	Round 1		4	4	3	4	5	3	5	6	5	4	3	4	5	6	4	2	3	4	74
USA	T87	Round 2		4	4	3	4	4	2	3	4	4	4	4	4	5	6	4	5	3	4	71 -145
Matteo Manassero	T91	Round 1		4	4	4	4	4	3	4	4	4	5	3	5	4	5	5	3	4	4	73
Italy	T87	Round 2		4	4	3	4	4	4	4	4	4	4	4	5	4	4	4	4	4	4	72 -145
Camilo Villegas	T51	Round 1		4	4	3	4	5	5	5	4	3	4	3	4	5	4	4	3	3	4	71
Colombia	T87	Round 2		4	4	3	4	3	3	4	5	4	5	5	4	5	6	4	3	4	4	74 -145
Alexander Noren	T18	Round 1		4	3	4	5	4	3	5	4	5	3	3	4	4	5	4	2	4	3	69
Sweden	T87	Round 2		4	4	3	5	3	4	5	4	5	6	4	4	3	5	5	2	5	5	76 -145
Robert Karlsson	T71	Round 1		5	4	3	4	5	3	5	4	3	4	3	3	5	5	4	3	5	4	72
Sweden	T94	Round 2		4	4	3	3	4	4	4	4	4	4	4	4	4	7	4	3	5	5	74 -146
Angel Cabrera	T71	Round 1		4	4	3	4	4	4	6	4	4	4	2	4	4	5	4	3	4	5	72
Argentina	T94	Round 2		4	4	4	5	3	4	4	5	4	4	2	6	4	5	6	3	4	3	74 -146
Luke Donald	T51	Round 1		4	4	2	4	4	4	4	4	4	4	4	4	5	5	5	3	3	4	71
England	T94	Round 2		5	4	4	5	4	3	4	4	4	4	3	4	3	5	5	4	5	5	75 -146
John Daly	T71	Round 1		3	4	3	5	5	3	4	4	4	4	3	5	5	5	4	3	4	4	72
USA	T94	Round 2		5	4	5	5	3	5	4	5	4	4	3	4	3	5	4	3	4	4	74 -146
Jason Dufner	T107	Round 1		5	6	3	4	5	4	5	4	4	4	3	4	4	4	4	3	3	5	74
USA	T94	Round 2		4	4	3	5	4	4	4	4	4	4	4	4	5	4	3	4	4	4	72 -146
Kevin Streelman	T141	Round 1		5	4	5	5	5	4	5	4	4	4	3	4	4	6	3	4	3	4	76
USA	T94	Round 2		4	4	3	4	4	3	4	5	4	5	3	4	3	5	5	3	4	3	70 -146
Neil Schietekat	T91	Round 1		5	4	4	4	5	4	6	4	3	4	3	4	4	4	4	2	4	5	73
South Africa	T94	Round 2		4	4	3	5	4	3	5	4	4	5	4	3	4	5	5	3	4	4	73 -146
Prom Meesawat	T71	Round 1		5	5	4	4	4	2	4	5	5	4	3	4	3	5	4	2	5	4	72
Thailand	T101	Round 2		4	4	3	4	3	3	4	6	4	4	3	4	4	7	5	3	5	5	75 -147
Martin Maritz	T91	Round 1		4	4	4	4	4	3	5	5	4	4	3	4	4	5	4	3	4	5	73
South Africa	T101	Round 2		4	5	3	5	4	4	4	4	5	5	4	5	4	5	4	3	4	3	74 -147
Lee Corfield	T71	Round 1		5	5	4	4	5	3	5	3	4	4	3	4	4	5	4	3	4	4	72
England	T101	Round 2		5	4	4	5	4	3	4	4	5	3	3	4	5	5	4	3	5	5	75 -147
Jason Knutzon	T126	Round 1		4	5	3	5	4	3	5	5	4	3	3	4	4	5	5	3	5	5	75
USA	T101	Round 2		4	4	4	4	5	3	4	6	4	3	3	4	5	4	3	4	4	4	72 -147
Charley Hoffman	T71	Round 1		4	4	3	4	4	3	5	5	4	4	3	4	4	5	4	3	4	5	72
USA	T101	Round 2		5	4	4	5	4	4	3	5	4	4	4	3	4	5	4	4	5	4	75 -147
Martin Laird	T71	Round 1		4	4	3	4	4	3	4	3	6	4	3	4	5	6	4	2	4	5	72
Scotland	T101	Round 2		5	4	3	5	4	3	4	4	4	5	3	4	4	5	4	3	5	6	75 -147
Geoff Ogilvy	T107	Round 1		5	4	3	4	4	5	4	4	4	5	3	4	3	6	5	2	4	5	74
Australia	T101	Round 2		4	4	3	4	4	3	5	5	4	6	3	4	3	5	4	3	5	4	73 -147
Ian Poulter	T18	Round 1		5	3	3	5	4	3	4	4	4	4	3	4	5	5	4	2	3	4	69
England	T101	Round 2		4	5	3	5	5	3	5	4	5	5	4	3	5	5	5	3	5	4	78 -147

HOLE			1	2	3	4	5	6	7	8	9	10	11	12	13	14	15	16	17	18	
PAR	POSITION		4	4	3	4	4	3	5	4	4	3	4	4	5	4	3	4	4	4	TOTAL
Thorbjorn Olesen Denmark	T91	Round 1	4	4	3	4	5	3	5	4	5	4	3	4	5	5	4	3	4	4	73
	T101	Round 2	5	4	3	4	4	4	3	5	5	4	3	4	4	6	4	3	4	5	74 -147
Lucas Bjerregaard* Denmark	T91	Round 1	4	4	3	4	5	3	5	5	6	4	3	4	4	5	4	2	5	3	73
	T110	Round 2	4	4	3	4	8	3	4	4	5	4	4	3	4	5	5	3	4	4	75 -148
Bernhard Langer Germany	T126	Round 1	4	5	3	4	4	3	4	5	8	5	3	4	4	5	4	2	4	4	75
	T110	Round 2	4	4	3	5	4	3	4	4	4	4	4	4	4	5	4	3	5	5	73 -148
Tadahiro Takayama Japan	T36	Round 1	4	4	3	5	4	3	4	4	5	3	3	4	6	4	3	4	3	4	70
	T110	Round 2	4	4	3	5	4	4	5	4	5	4	4	4	4	5	5	3	5	6	78 -148
SM Bae Korea	T71	Round 1	5	4	4	4	5	4	4	4	4	3	3	5	4	5	3	4	3	4	72
	T110	Round 2	3	3	3	5	5	4	5	7	6	4	3	4	4	5	4	3	4	4	76 -148
Robert Garrigus USA	T107	Round 1	4	4	4	4	4	3	4	4	6	4	3	4	5	5	3	3	5	5	74
	T110	Round 2	4	5	3	4	4	3	4	4	5	4	4	4	4	4	3	5	5	5	74 -148
Mark Calcavecchia USA	T18	Round 1	4	4	3	3	4	3	4	4	4	4	4	3	4	5	4	3	4	5	69
	T110	Round 2	6	5	3	7	4	4	5	4	4	4	5	3	3	5	4	4	5	4	79 -148
Francesco Molinari Italy	T91	Round 1	4	5	3	5	4	3	4	4	4	4	4	4	4	4	4	4	4	5	73
	T110	Round 2	4	4	3	4	5	3	5	6	4	4	4	4	4	5	4	3	4	5	75 -148
Tetsuji Hiratsuka Japan	T126	Round 1	5	4	3	4	5	3	6	5	4	4	4	5	5	5	4	3	3	4	75
	T110	Round 2	4	4	4	5	5	2	4	3	5	4	3	4	4	5	4	3	5	5	73 -148
Ernie Els South Africa	T71	Round 1	4	4	3	4	5	3	4	6	5	4	3	4	4	4	4	3	4	4	72
	T110	Round 2	5	4	4	5	3	6	5	4	4	4	4	4	4	4	4	3	5	4	76 -148
Sandy Lyle Scotland	T91	Round 1	4	4	3	5	4	3	5	3	5	5	3	4	5	4	4	2	5	5	73
	T119	Round 2	4	4	3	5	5	4	3	4	6	4	6	3	4	5	5	3	4	3	76 -149
Jonathan Byrd USA	T126	Round 1	5	4	4	4	4	3	4	5	5	4	4	5	4	5	4	3	4	4	75
	T119	Round 2	4	3	4	5	4	2	6	5	4	4	3	4	4	5	5	3	4	5	74 -149
Kurt Barnes Australia	T6	Round 1	5	4	3	4	4	3	4	4	4	4	4	3	3	4	4	3	4	4	68
	T119	Round 2	4	6	4	6	4	6	6	5	4	4	3	4	4	4	5	3	4	5	81 -149
Brad Kennedy Australia	T146	Round 1	4	4	4	4	4	4	5	4	4	4	4	3	4	8	4	3	5	5	77
	T119	Round 2	4	3	2	4	5	3	4	6	4	5	4	4	5	4	4	3	4	4	72 -149
Kevin Na USA	T107	Round 1	4	4	4	4	4	3	4	5	5	5	3	5	5	5	4	3	4	3	74
	T119	Round 2	6	4	2	5	4	4	5	5	4	4	4	4	4	4	4	3	5	4	75 -149
Mark Laskey Wales	T91	Round 1	4	4	3	5	4	2	5	5	5	4	4	4	5	4	3	4	3	5	73
	T119	Round 2	5	4	3	6	4	3	4	5	5	6	3	4	4	5	4	3	4	4	76 -149
Scott Jamieson Scotland	T126	Round 1	5	4	2	4	5	3	5	4	4	4	3	5	5	6	4	3	5	4	75
	T125	Round 2	5	4	3	5	4	3	5	4	5	4	3	4	4	7	4	2	4	5	75 -150
Steve Marino USA	T107	Round 1	5	4	3	3	4	3	5	4	4	4	4	5	4	6	5	3	4	4	74
	T125	Round 2	4	4	3	4	5	3	4	5	4	5	4	4	4	5	5	3	4	6	76 -150
Nathan Green Australia	T107	Round 1	3	5	4	4	5	3	4	6	4	5	3	4	3	5	5	2	4	5	74
	T125	Round 2	4	4	4	5	4	3	5	6	4	4	4	4	3	6	4	3	5	4	76 -150
Aaron Baddeley Australia	T146	Round 1	4	4	3	5	4	4	4	4	5	5	4	4	7	4	4	4	4	4	77
	T125	Round 2	4	5	3	5	3	3	4	4	4	5	3	4	4	6	4	4	4	4	73 -150
Thomas Shadbolt England	T107	Round 1	5	4	4	4	5	3	5	4	4	4	4	3	5	5	4	3	4	4	74
	T125	Round 2	3	5	4	5	4	5	5	4	4	5	5	3	4	5	4	3	4	4	76 -150
Simon Lilly England	T107	Round 1	5	4	3	4	5	3	5	4	6	4	3	4	3	5	4	3	5	4	74
	T125	Round 2	5	5	3	6	4	4	5	5	4	4	4	4	4	5	4	3	3	4	76 -150
Chris Tidland USA	T146	Round 1	5	4	3	5	5	4	5	4	4	4	2	3	5	6	5	4	4	5	77
	T125	Round 2	5	4	3	5	4	5	4	4	4	4	3	4	4	5	3	3	5	4	73 -150
Matt Kuchar USA	T107	Round 1	4	5	4	4	5	3	5	4	5	4	3	3	4	5	4	3	4	5	74
	T132	Round 2	5	4	4	4	4	3	5	5	3	4	4	6	4	5	4	4	4	5	77 -151

	POSITION	Round	1	2	3	4	5	6	7	8	9	10	11	12	13	14	15	16	17	18	TOTAL
PAR			4	4	3	4	4	3	5	4	4	4	4	3	4	4	5	4	3	4	4
Chih-Bing Lam Singapore	T141 **T132**	Round 1 Round 2	4 4	5 5	4 4	4 5	4 4	3 4	4 4	5 5	4 4	5 5	2 3	4 4	4 4	6 4	4 5	4 4	5 3	5 4	76 75-151
Thongchai Jaidee Thailand	T126 **T132**	Round 1 Round 2	4 5	4 4	3 3	5 6	4 4	3 4	6 5	4 5	5 4	4 5	4 4	3 3	5 3	4 4	4 5	3 3	5 4	5 5	75 76-151
Hiroyuki Fujita Japan	T126 **T132**	Round 1 Round 2	4 4	4 4	2 3	4 5	4 4	3 3	6 5	4 4	4 3	5 5	3 3	4 5	4 4	5 7	5 4	4 3	5 4	5 6	75 76-151
Ben Curtis USA	T146 **T132**	Round 1 Round 2	4 4	4 5	3 3	4 4	5 5	3 4	6 4	5 5	5 4	5 4	3 3	5 4	5 4	4 5	4 4	4 3	3 5	5 4	77 74-151
Brian Davis England	T126 **T132**	Round 1 Round 2	4 4	4 4	4 4	5 5	4 4	3 3	5 4	5 5	5 4	5 5	3 3	4 4	4 4	5 5	3 5	3 4	4 5	5 4	75 76-151
Mark O'Meara USA	T141 **T138**	Round 1 Round 2	4 5	5 4	5 4	4 4	4 4	3 3	5 5	4 4	4 5	3 4	3 4	5 5	5 4	5 6	5 4	4 3	4 4	4 4	76 76-152
KT Kim Korea	T126 **T138**	Round 1 Round 2	4 5	4 4	3 4	4 6	5 4	3 3	6 5	4 4	4 4	5 5	3 4	5 5	5 4	4 5	4 3	3 4	5 4	4 4	75 77-152
Bob Estes USA	T107 **T138**	Round 1 Round 2	5 4	4 5	4 4	4 5	5 4	3 4	5 5	5 5	5 4	4 4	3 3	3 5	4 4	5 6	4 4	2 3	4 4	5 5	74 78-152
Adam Wootton England	T51 **T141**	Round 1 Round 2	4 5	4 4	2 3	5 4	4 5	2 7	5 4	4 6	4 4	3 5	4 3	4 4	6 5	4 5	5 5	3 3	4 5	4 5	71 82-153
Andrew Johnston England	T107 **T141**	Round 1 Round 2	4 5	4 4	3 4	4 5	5 4	2 3	4 5	3 5	5 5	4 5	4 3	4 4	7 3	6 7	4 5	3 3	3 5	5 4	74 79-153
Jerry Kelly USA	T107 **T141**	Round 1 Round 2	5 4	6 4	3 3	4 5	4 5	4 3	6 5	4 5	4 4	3 4	2 4	5 4	4 4	5 5	4 6	3 5	4 5	4 4	74 79-153
Prayad Marksaeng Thailand	T141 **T141**	Round 1 Round 2	5 5	5 4	4 3	4 4	4 4	3 3	6 5	4 5	5 4	3 5	3 5	4 4	4 5	6 6	5 4	3 3	3 4	5 4	76 77-153
Rhys Davies Wales	T126 **T141**	Round 1 Round 2	6 4	5 5	2 4	4 5	4 4	3 4	5 4	4 5	4 4	4 4	4 4	4 4	5 3	5 7	4 5	3 4	4 4	5 4	75 78-153
Francis McGuirk England	T146 **T141**	Round 1 Round 2	5 5	5 4	3 3	6 5	4 4	3 3	5 5	5 5	4 4	4 5	4 3	5 4	5 3	5 5	4 5	2 4	4 4	4 5	77 76-153
Andy Smith England	154 **T147**	Round 1 Round 2	5 5	4 3	4 4	4 4	5 5	3 2	5 4	5 5	5 4	4 4	5 4	4 3	4 4	7 5	4 4	3 3	5 5	5 5	81 73-154
Alvaro Quiros Spain	T126 **T147**	Round 1 Round 2	4 4	4 4	2 3	5 5	4 4	3 3	3 5	6 6	4 5	5 5	3 4	4 4	5 4	7 5	4 5	5 4	3 5	4 4	75 79-154
Ryo Ishikawa Japan	T107 **T147**	Round 1 Round 2	5 5	4 3	4 3	4 5	4 4	4 3	7 4	4 5	5 5	3 4	4 4	3 5	4 6	4 6	4 6	3 3	4 4	4 5	74 80-154
Hiroo Kawai Japan	T126 **T150**	Round 1 Round 2	5 4	4 4	3 4	5 5	4 5	3 3	4 5	5 4	5 5	4 5	3 4	4 4	4 4	5 7	5 4	3 3	5 5	4 5	75 80-155
David Duval USA	153 **T150**	Round 1 Round 2	4 5	4 4	3 4	4 6	5 4	4 3	6 4	5 6	5 5	3 4	4 4	3 4	6 3	5 6	4 4	3 3	5 4	5 4	78 77-155
Todd Hamilton USA	T146 **152**	Round 1 Round 2	4 5	4 4	3 3	4 4	4 4	3 3	7 5	5 4	5 7	5 4	3 4	5 4	4 4	5 5	5 5	3 5	4 5	4 4	77 79-156
Markus Brier Austria	T146 **153**	Round 1 Round 2	4 4	4 5	3 4	5 4	4 4	4 3	4 4	4 5	4 5	4 4	3 4	5 6	5 4	5 6	6 4	3 3	4 6	6 5	77 80-157
Simon Edwards Wales	T155 **154**	Round 1 Round 2	6 4	5 5	4 4	5 5	5 3	4 4	6 4	4 5	5 4	4 5	4 3	4 5	5 5	4 5	4 5	4 4	4 5	5 4	82 79-161
Craig Hinton* England	T155 **155**	Round 1 Round 2	5 6	5 6	3 5	4 8	8 4	3 3	6 6	5 4	4 5	5 3	3 3	4 4	5 5	5 8	3 5	4 4	5 4	5 4	82 87-169
Retief Goosen South Africa	**156**	Round 1	4	3	4	4	5	3	5	4	5	4	4	5	5	5	4	3	4	5	76 **WD**

THE TOP TENS

Eagles/Birdies

1. George Coetzee 0/16
1. Dustin Johnson 1/15
1. *Darren Clarke 2/14*
4. Charl Schwartzel 0/15
5. Thomas Bjorn 0/14
5. Chad Campbell 0/14
5. Gary Woodland 0/14
8. Anthony Kim 0/13
8. Steve Stricker 0/13
8. Fredrik Jacobson............1/12

Pars

1. Webb Simpson 54
2. Lucas Glover.....................53
2. Adam Scott.......................53
4. Rickie Fowler 52
4. Pablo Larrazabal 52
4. Gregory Bourdy..................52
7. Miguel Angel Jimenez........51
8. Charles Howell III 50
8. Bubba Watson 50
8. Trevor Immelman...............50
37. Darren Clarke 44

Bogeys

1. Stephen Gallacher.........22
2. Jim Furyk 21
2. Edoardo Molinari................21
4. Floris De Vries 20
4. Rory Sabbatini....................20
4. Louis Oosthuizen................20
4. Bo Van Pelt 20
4. Paul Lawrie 20
4. Jung-Gon Hwang 20
10. 5 players tied 19
81. Darren Clarke 11

Double Bogeys/Worse

1. Henrik Stenson............7/0
1. Jung-Gon Hwang 6/1
3. Craig Hinton.....................3/3
4. Alvaro Quiros...................4/0
4. Marcus Brier....................4/0
4. Kenneth Ferrie 2/2
7. 3 players tied 3/0
7. 4 players tied 2/1
7. Mark Wilson 1/2
68. Darren Clarke 1/0

Driving Distance

1. Dustin Johnson.........334.9
2. Bubba Watson................332.1
3. Gary Woodland 325.0
4. Bo Van Pelt 324.8
5. Seung-Yul Noh 322.3
6. Jason Day 321.5
7. Ryan Palmer.................319.9
8. Webb SImpson..............316.8
9. Rickie Fowler 315.6
9. Kyle Stanley..................315.6
17. Darren Clarke 311.8

Fairways Hit

Maximum of 56

1. YE Yang 38
2. Davis Love III 35
2. Trevor Immelman..............35
4. Richard Green 34
4. Gregory Havret.................34
6. Thomas Bjorn 33
6. Tom Lehman.....................33
6. Anders Hansen.................33
9. Jeff Overton.....................32
9. Rory Sabbatini..................32
9. Kenneth Ferrie 32
56. Darren Clarke 23

Greens in Regulation

Maximum of 72

1. Davis Love III 54
2. Darren Clarke 51
3. Phil Mickelson 50
4. Lucas Glover......................49
5. Richard Green 48
6. Dustin Johnson 47
7. George Coetzee 46
7. Bubba Watson 46
7. Jeff Overton......................46
10. YE Yang............................45
10. Gary Woodland 45

Putts

1. Raphael Jacquelin........ 109
1. Steve Stricker 109
3. Webb Simpson.................. 111
3. Stewart Cink 111
5. Thomas Bjorn 113
5. Anthony Kim..................... 113
5. Ryan Moore...................... 113
5. Yuta Ikeda....................... 113
9. Chad Campbell 114
9. Simon Dyson.................... 114
31. Darren Clarke 119

Statistical Rankings

	Driving Distance	Rank	Fairways Hit	Rank	Greens In Regulation	Rank	Putts	Rank
Robert Allenby	289.4	55	28	28	34	68	120	36
Fredrik Andersson Hed	294.5	50	20	69	37	54	120	36
Ricky Barnes	309.4	22	27	35	42	27	122	44
Thomas Bjorn	304.8	33	33	6	41	30	113	5
Gregory Bourdy	286.1	59	27	35	35	64	115	11
Gary Boyd	307.5	25	24	49	40	42	122	44
Chad Campbell	302.3	39	25	44	43	17	114	9
Paul Casey	300.4	42	28	28	36	59	119	31
KJ Choi	300.5	41	25	44	39	47	117	19
Stewart Cink	287.5	57	29	23	35	64	111	3
Darren Clarke	311.8	17	23	56	51	2	119	31
George Coetzee	299.8	44	24	49	46	7	120	36
Jason Day	321.5	6	23	56	37	54	116	14
Floris De Vries	297.5	47	29	23	42	27	124	55
Simon Dyson	303.5	34	22	60	42	27	114	9
Kenneth Ferrie	295.1	49	32	9	37	54	125	60
Rickie Fowler	315.6	9	25	44	44	12	116	14
Harrison Frazar	309.5	20	27	35	40	42	127	66
Jim Furyk	286.6	58	27	35	37	54	119	31
Stephen Gallacher	284.0	63	24	49	36	59	121	42
Sergio Garcia	299.6	45	23	56	41	30	115	11
Lucas Glover	312.4	15	28	28	49	4	124	55
Richard Green	292.9	52	34	4	48	5	126	62
Bill Haas	300.4	42	30	16	40	42	124	55
Anders Hansen	305.4	31	33	6	41	30	118	26
Gregory Havret	299.1	46	34	4	38	52	116	14
Charles Howell III	309.5	20	28	28	44	12	125	60
Jung-Gon Hwang	277.5	69	27	35	31	71	117	19
Yuta Ikeda	282.8	65	22	60	39	47	113	5
Trevor Immelman	305.5	30	35	2	41	30	122	44
Fredrik Jacobson	311.9	16	24	49	41	30	117	19
Raphael Jacqueline	291.8	53	29	23	37	54	109	1
Miguel Angel Jimenez	279.0	68	28	28	39	47	117	19
Dustin Johnson	334.9	1	28	28	47	6	116	14
Zach Johnson	283.5	64	31	12	43	17	117	19
Martin Kaymer	305.4	31	30	16	43	17	115	11
Simon Khan	289.1	56	29	23	43	17	122	44
Anthony Kim	312.9	13	24	49	43	17	113	5
Pablo Larrazabal	276.8	70	25	44	39	47	119	31
Paul Lawrie	285.0	61	22	60	35	64	122	44
Tom Lehman	285.4	60	33	6	43	17	122	44
Spencer Levin	307.3	27	31	12	40	42	116	14
Tom Lewis*	307.8	23	24	49	41	30	122	44
Davis Love III	273.3	71	35	2	54	1	130	70
Joost Luiten	296.6	48	27	35	41	30	126	62
Richard McEvoy	311.8	17	27	35	38	52	123	52
Rory McIlroy	311.0	19	28	28	43	17	120	36
Phil Mickelson	307.3	27	27	35	50	3	122	44
Matthew Millar	280.5	67	30	16	34	68	118	26
Edoardo Molinari	303.1	36	29	23	41	30	126	62
Ryan Moore	307.4	26	30	16	36	59	113	5
Seung-Yul Noh	322.3	5	21	68	44	12	123	52
Louis Oosthuizen	301.1	40	25	44	34	68	118	26
Jeff Overton	314.8	11	32	9	46	7	128	68
Ryan Palmer	319.9	7	22	60	41	30	120	36
Robert Rock	307.8	23	24	49	41	30	120	36
Justin Rose	302.5	38	31	12	43	17	126	62
Rory Sabbatini	314.8	11	32	9	44	12	132	71
Charl Schwartzel	302.9	37	31	12	44	12	119	31
Adam Scott	284.8	62	27	35	41	30	118	26
Webb Simpson	316.8	8	30	16	40	42	111	3
Kyle Stanley	315.6	9	23	56	43	17	124	55
Henrik Stenson	303.4	35	22	60	35	64	118	26
Steve Stricker	282.3	66	30	16	36	59	109	1
Peter Uihlein*	305.8	29	18	71	41	30	124	55
Bo Van Pelt	324.8	4	22	60	43	17	127	66
Bubba Watson	332.1	2	22	60	46	7	128	68
Tom Watson	294.4	51	22	60	39	47	117	19
Mark Wilson	291.0	54	30	16	36	59	117	19
Gary Woodland	325.0	3	20	69	45	10	123	52
YE Yang	312.5	14	38	1	45	10	121	42

NON QUALIFIERS AFTER 36 HOLES

Player	Driving Distance	Rank	Fairways Hit	Rank	Greens In Regulation	Rank	Putts	Rank
Thomas Aiken	313.0	40	11	117	20	86	59	54
Aaron Baddeley	299.0	96	15	33	15	139	58	38
SM Bae	315.3	29	18	5	23	32	61	91
Kurt Barnes	315.8	27	9	141	18	114	57	21
Lucas Bjerregaard*	314.3	36	7	150	22	46	64	132
Markus Brier	280.0	144	10	131	12	151	58	38
Jonathan Byrd	305.0	77	11	117	19	104	63	119
Angel Cabrera	314.5	35	12	92	18	114	58	38
Mark Calcavecchia	301.8	86	14	50	21	66	62	104
Aiejandro Canizares	293.8	119	14	50	25	8	61	91
Lee Corfield	301.8	86	6	152	21	66	63	119
Ben Crane	301.8	86	16	19	20	86	61	91
Ben Curtis	276.3	149	15	33	20	86	65	140
John Daly	308.5	57	10	131	20	86	62	104
Rhys Davies	291.8	123	15	33	17	126	63	119
Brian Davis	303.8	82	16	19	20	86	66	146
Luke Donald	293.0	121	16	19	21	66	62	104
Jason Dufner	325.5	12	14	50	23	32	63	119
David Duval	301.0	91	10	131	13	147	60	71
Simon Edwards	310.8	48	13	72	12	151	67	150
Ernie Els	295.5	114	13	72	19	104	62	104
Bob Estes	306.5	67	12	92	18	114	65	140
Ross Fisher	319.0	19	13	72	17	126	55	9
Hiroyuki Fujita	290.5	124	9	141	13	147	58	38
Robert Garrigus	330.3	5	10	131	21	66	60	71
Nathan Green	309.5	51	12	92	17	126	59	54
Todd Hamilton	309.0	55	12	92	14	146	60	71
Peter Hanson	308.3	58	13	72	21	66	61	91
Padraig Harrington	296.3	108	5	155	22	46	61	91
Craig Hinton*	297.5	104	6	152	13	147	68	152
Tetsuji Hiratsuka	279.0	147	15	33	17	126	59	54
Charley Hoffman	320.0	18	13	72	22	46	63	119
JB Holmes	334.0	3	13	72	21	66	57	21
Ryo Ishikawa	296.5	107	15	33	11	154	56	14
Thongchai Jaidee	311.0	45	12	92	21	66	68	152
Scott Jamieson	316.8	22	13	72	21	66	65	140
Andrew Johnston	308.0	60	9	141	19	104	63	119
Robert Karlsson	306.3	69	15	33	23	32	62	104
Hiroo Kawai	282.5	139	13	72	18	114	67	150
Jerry Kelly	287.8	133	18	5	16	135	60	71
Brad Kennedy	303.3	83	18	5	18	114	61	91
KT Kim	305.5	74	15	33	11	154	57	21
Jason Knutzon	298.8	98	16	19	15	139	57	21
Matt Kuchar	305.8	73	14	50	18	114	64	132
Rick Kulacz	297.8	101	11	117	20	86	59	54
Martin Laird	320.3	17	6	152	22	46	61	91
Chih-Bing Lam	305.0	77	14	50	17	126	63	119
Bernhard Langer	280.3	143	14	50	25	8	65	140
Mark Laskey	316.3	25	11	117	15	139	59	54
Justin Leonard	297.5	104	16	19	22	46	62	104
Simon Lilly	295.8	112	9	141	24	16	69	155
Sandy Lyle	296.3	108	11	117	20	86	61	91
Bryden Macpherson*	281.5	142	14	50	19	104	58	38
Hunter Mahan	283.8	136	12	92	22	46	62	104
Matteo Manassero	280.0	144	11	117	18	114	58	38
Steve Marino	294.3	117	14	50	16	135	63	119
Martin Maritz	306.3	69	14	50	15	139	57	21
Prayad Marksaeng	299.0	96	12	92	16	135	64	132
Graeme McDowell	326.5	10	11	117	22	46	60	71
Francis McGuirk	305.5	74	8	148	19	104	65	140
Prom Meesawat	274.3	151	11	117	15	139	54	4
Francesco Molinari	300.3	92	18	5	19	104	61	91
Kevin Na	313.8	38	14	50	20	86	64	132
Alexander Noren	329.8	6	16	19	21	66	61	91
Sean O'Hair	325.0	13	12	92	20	86	57	21
Mark O'Meara	296.3	108	15	33	15	139	62	104
Geoff Ogilvy	288.8	130	15	33	12	151	52	1
Thorbjorn Olesen	336.8	1	14	50	19	104	60	71
Ian Poulter	292.0	122	9	141	20	86	64	132
Alvaro Quiros	316.8	22	13	72	15	139	61	91
Neil Schietekat	307.0	65	11	117	13	147	54	4
Thomas Shadbolt	301.8	86	11	117	19	104	63	119
Andy Smith	294.0	118	12	92	17	126	64	132
Brandt Snedeker	306.0	72	17	11	22	46	62	104
Graeme Storm	282.5	139	17	11	24	16	64	132
Kevin Streelman	307.8	62	12	92	17	126	60	71
Tadahiro Takayama	309.0	55	13	72	22	46	66	146
Chris Tidland	282.5	139	15	33	16	135	62	104
Camilo Villegas	297.8	101	17	11	18	114	57	21
Nick Watney	304.0	81	8	148	18	114	58	38
Lee Westwood	315.3	29	13	72	29	1	68	152
Peter Whiteford	305.0	77	16	19	25	8	66	146
Danny Willett	311.0	45	14	50	21	66	60	71
Adam Wootton	285.5	135	15	33	17	126	60	71

PHOTOGRAPHY CREDITS

David Cannon – front cover, 8-9, 10, 12, 13, 14, 16, 24 top, 25, 27 top (2), 32 (2), 35 bottom, 36 top, 38, 41, 42, 50 top, 70, 74 top, 76 top right, 78 left, 82, 102 top right, 107 left, 109 (2), 110 right

Stanley Chou – 20 top left

Tom Dulat – 21 top right

Stuart Franklin – 28 top, 30, 31 bottom left, 37, 51 bottom, 62, 65 (2), 76 top left, 80 top left, 86 bottom, 87, 88 bottom, 89, 90 left, 90 bottom right, 91, 96 top left, 97, 100 top left, 107 middle, 108 (3), 111, 112 top, 112 bottom left, 113

Scott Halleran – 26, 27 bottom, 31 top, 33 top, 33 bottom right, 54, 59 bottom, 69 bottom, 71 bottom, 80 top right, 93, 95 top left, 99 right, 100 bottom, 107 right, 114

Ross Kinnaird – 6, 19 far left, 19 far right, 28 bottom, 34, 35 top, 40, 51 top, 73, 74 bottom, 79, 81, 84, 95 top right, 96 right, 110 left, 104-105

Streeter Lecka – 75, 94

Matthew Lewis – 22, 36 bottom, 39, 46, 49 bottom, 56, 57, 58, 60, 66, 77, 100 middle left, 102 bottom

Warren Little – 19 second left, 19 second right, 21 bottom left, 24 bottom, 69 top, 78 right, 80 bottom, 92, 100 top right, 103

Hunter Martin – 20 top right

Robert Prezioso – 20 bottom

Andrew Redington – 29, 31 bottom right, 33 bottom left, 44, 48, 49 top, 50 bottom, 52 (2), 53, 59 top, 61, 67, 85, 86 top, 95 bottom, 98

Ian Walton – back cover, 47, 55, 64, 68, 71 top, 76 bottom, 88 top, 90 top right, 96 bottom left, 99 left, 101, 102 top left, 112 bottom right

THE ROYAL
ST GEORGE'S GOLF CLUB
SANDWICH